HAUNTED HOSPITALS

MARK LESLIE
RHONDA PARRISH

HAUNTED HOSPITALS

Eerie Tales About Hospitals, Sanatoriums, and Other Institutions

DUNDURN
TORONTO

Cover image: ©123rf.com/boscorelli
Printer: Webcom

Library and Archives Canada Cataloguing in Publication

Leslie, Mark, 1969-, author
     Haunted hospitals : eerie tales about hospitals, sanatoriums, and other institutions /
Mark Leslie and Rhonda Parrish.

Includes bibliographical references.
Issued in print and electronic formats.
ISBN 978-1-4597-3786-0 (paperback).--ISBN 978-1-4597-3787-7 (pdf).--
ISBN 978-1-4597-3788-4 (epub)

     1. Haunted hospitals. 2. Haunted places. 3. Ghosts. I. Parrish, Rhonda, author II. Title.

BF1474.4.L47 2017   133.1'22   C2016-907193-6
                                                                  C2016-907194-4

1   2   3   4   5   21   20   19   18   17

We acknowledge the support of the **Canada Council for the Arts,** which last year invested $153 million to bring the arts to Canadians throughout the country, and the **Ontario Arts Council** for our publishing program. We also acknowledge the financial support of the **Government of Ontario,** through the **Ontario Book Publishing Tax Credit** and the **Ontario Media Development Corporation,** and the **Government of Canada.**

Nous remercions le **Conseil des arts du Canada** de son soutien. L'an dernier, le Conseil a investi 153 millions de dollars pour mettre de l'art dans la vie des Canadiennes et des Canadiens de tout le pays.

Care has been taken to trace the ownership of copyright material used in this book. The author and the publisher welcome any information enabling them to rectify any references or credits in subsequent editions.
                                                                  — *J. Kirk Howard, President*

The publisher is not responsible for websites or their content unless they are owned by the publisher.

Printed and bound in Canada.

VISIT US AT

dundurn.com | @dundurnpress | dundurnpress | dundurnpress

Dundurn
3 Church Street, Suite 500
Toronto, Ontario, Canada
M5E 1M2

Rhonda dedicates this book to those who labour in the medical field. Whether you work on the front lines helping those who are unwell or injured, or stay in the shadows striving to improve treatments or find cures, this book is for you.

Mark dedicates this book to Dr. Sean Costello, who has dedicated much of his life not only to the medical profession but also to being a father. Sean, your writing mentorship and your friendship are priceless gifts.

CONTENTS

HAUNTED HOSPITALS, ASYLUMS, AND PSYCHIATRIC INSTITUTIONS

CANADA

Alberta

THE UNITED STATES

REST OF THE WORLD

THE SLEEPWALKING DEAD: A CAUTIONARY TALE

HAUNTED PRISONS

CANADA

THE UNITED STATES

REST OF THE WORLD

Abandoned or otherwise, hospitals sometimes inspire fear and urban legends.

A NOTE FROM THE AUTHORS

During our research we encountered many hospitals, abandoned or other-wise, that give people chills, inspire a feeling of being watched, or feature in local ghost stories and urban legends. Many of those stories were shared directly with us by witnesses who had either directly experienced some-thing or had heard about a happening first-hand from a trusted colleague or relative. In other cases tales published in magazines, newspaper articles, books, or via special interest groups who collect and share ghostly anec-dotes led us to hours of research.

As with virtually every ghost story shared, the story is based upon a kernel of factual evidence, documented experiences, and historical detail. Stories are combined and layered for generations as they are passed on verbally, written about in various print and online sources, and also shared on local tours or ghost walks of the region.

Sometimes in our research we encountered conflicting details from previous documentation; wherever we encountered such crossroads, we have attempted to portray the stories as plainly as possible so that you, the reader, might make your own judgment.

At other times, in the interest of wrapping the kernel of truth within a captivating and alluring tale of speculative wonder, we have played upon the unknown, the mysterious, thus allowing you to fall under the spell that a magnificent historical location can sometimes have upon a person.

We hope you enjoy the balance we have reached between those two extremes.

Some of the stories you will read are lengthy, detailed, and rich with content.

Unfortunately, though, we could not always track down enough information about a location to elaborate further. In the interest of ensuring your awareness of these locations, however, we thought it better to include what brief elements we had uncovered than to ignore these places completely.

When first approaching this project we considered writing about hospitals, asylums, and prisons; and as the work and research began, we realized that the book might easily double in length if we kept at our original trajectory.

There is such an interesting crossover among hospitals, asylums, and prisons that we didn't want to abandon the prisons altogether, particularly in cases where it's difficult to determine the historic building's main significance. In the end we decided to focus the majority of the book's content on hospitals and psychiatric institutions, but we have included a section acknowledging some very haunted prisons that found cross-purposes as asylums.

INTRODUCTION

"I live near a haunted hospital."

We were in a busy room in the middle of a bustling convention — a convention where, as one of the guests of honour, Mark had plenty of demands on his time and attention. Still, as soon as I said those six words, I had Mark's undivided attention. Which, I won't lie, had totally been my intent. From that moment on this book was inevitable. Actually, come to think of it, this book has been inevitable from the moment I saw the abandoned Charles Camsell Hospital.

My husband and I had just bought our very first house. It all happened in kind of a rush, and the only research we'd had time to do was ask an Edmonton community on LiveJournal about the neighbourhood (back when LiveJournal was still relevant).

It was autumn twilight when we first returned to the house — *our* house — to bask in the glow of new home ownership. Purple shadows stretched across the streets and trees shook nearly naked limbs at us in the gusty breeze. As our family of three drove up to the corner, we looked west, and there it was — a huge institutional building looming over us. There were no lights in or around it, just a dark, menacing silhouette squatting down the street from our new home.

I don't know how we hadn't seen it before, but we hadn't. And none of us knew what it could be. My first thought was a jail. My husband

The former Charles Camsell Hospital: The huge, institutional-looking abandoned building.

reckoned hospital. Our daughter, who was six at the time, didn't have a guess; she just thought it was cool.

My husband turned out to be correct. The ominous structure looming on our street was the decommissioned Charles Camsell Hospital.

The building fascinated me. It took a lot of willpower not to go exploring, and I had to constantly remind myself that I was a grown-up who ought not to go sneaking around empty buildings in search of a way in. A *lot* of willpower. Just a couple months later, when I first heard it referred to as the "haunted hospital," my curiosity grew exponentially.

I've never been inside the Charles Camsell Hospital, but it continues to captivate my imagination. It forms the setting in some of my written work and frequently stars in the stories I tell only to myself. I'd long planned to write something non-fiction about it, and then I met Mark, and things just clicked into place. Serendipity.

Now, I come to the paranormal from a very skeptical place. (If you feel as though the words "allegedly," "apparently," and "reportedly" are overused in this book, that's on me. Sorry, not sorry). But I believe in energy and I love a good spooky story. And there's something else, too ...

Last week we said goodbye to our beloved family dog. Tre was twelve when he died and he'd been a part of our family since he was eight weeks old. In the days immediately following his passing, I heard him. Twice. The first was the unmistakable clattering sound he always made as he clumsily jumped off the foot of my bed, his nails scratching against the hardwood. The second was the click-clack sound of him walking across the tiled kitchen floor. I'm sure what I heard was the result of imagination, wishful thinking, and memory, but what if —?

That's the question that fascinates me, skeptical or not. Because there are so many things we don't know for sure, *what if...?*

If paranormal phenomena are going to occur, what better place than in a hospital? Day after day the most extreme of human experiences play out within the walls of hospitals. The most intense emotions are experienced again and again. Birth. Death. Trauma. Suffering. If paranormal activity is tied to energy or emotions, hospitals are the perfect petri dishes in which to culture it.

Furthermore, if human spirits are trapped on this earth by trauma, disturbance, or unfinished business, again, what better location than a hospital to forge the chains that hold them here?

In this book, Mark and I retell several stories, legends, and real-life encounters that take place at hospitals in Canada, the United States, and all over the world. We've got eerie tales of abandoned tuberculosis hospitals whose hallways are teeming with shadow people, and childlike spirits trapped within the walls of a sanatorium whose only entertainment comes from playing ball with paranormal investigators. There are stories about full-bodied apparitions, disembodied voices, and spirits physically attacking those who dare to trespass on their territory.

I live near a haunted hospital. I can take a walk and check it out any time I want. Not everyone is that lucky, so throughout this book Mark and I wanted to bring the stories of haunted hospitals to you. And maybe raise a few hairs on the back of your neck because, really, *what if...?*

— *Rhonda Parrish*

A WORD ABOUT
PSYCHIATRIC TREATMENTS

Throughout the course of this book we talk about psychiatric hospitals, wards, and asylums, and as a part of that discussion we frequently mention treatments that, to our modern sensibilities, seem more like cruel and unusual punishments than therapeutic procedures. We want to emphasize, however, that in their time these were considered cutting-edge therapies that benefited patients. The people performing these procedures were not, for the most part, sadistic or evil, but were truly trying to help. In fact, some of these practices have proven effective enough that their use continues, in one form or another, even to this day.

One such example is electroconvulsive therapy, which is the current term for the procedure formerly known as electroshock therapy (or just shock therapy). Electroconvulsive therapy, or ECT, involves passing small electrical currents through the brain. This causes a brief seizure and also seems to change brain chemistry, and the technique remains in use to help people with extreme or treatment-resistant depression. In the past high doses of electricity were used, and the patient was not given any anaesthesia. This brutal version of ECT was immortalized in *One Flew Over the Cuckoo's Nest*, and several other books and films, and frequently lead to memory loss, broken bones, and permanent brain damage. Today

ECT is performed using small electric currents while the patient is under general anaesthesia — not nearly so dramatic or damaging.

Still, no matter how good the medical personnel's intentions might have been, we don't want to minimize how traumatic and terrifying these treatments would have been for the patient. Undergoing trepanation (drilling or scraping a hole in the skull), transorbital lobotomies (inserting a tool that resembles an ice pick through a patient's eye socket and into the brain), ECT without anaesthesia, or insulin shock therapy would have been nothing short of a nightmare — especially for a patient already plagued with mental health issues. One must assume that this kind of fear, pain, and trauma affected not only the people involved, but also the energy of the places where they occurred.

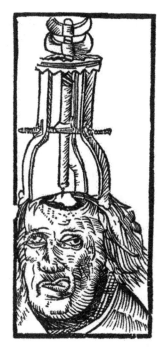

A 1525 engraving by Peter Treveris, showing a trepanation operation, from Hieronymus Braunschweig's Buch der Cirrugia.

A WORD ABOUT SANATORIUMS AND THE WHITE PLAGUE

We'll be dealing with a variety of different types of hospitals in this book. For the most part the nature of the hospital is obvious from its name — military hospital, prison hospital, psychiatric hospital — but one term you may not be familiar with is *sanatorium*. A sanatorium is a hospital for the treatment of chronic diseases, most frequently tuberculosis.

In order to understand the kinds of hauntings experienced in sanatoriums, it's important to know a little about the history of tuberculosis and how it has been treated in the past. Tuberculosis, also called consumption because of the serious weight loss in those who are afflicted, is known as the white plague. As with any disease that has been around for hundreds of years, some of the treatments for tuberculosis sound almost worse than the disease itself.

The best example of this is thoracoplasty. In the words of Josh, a tour guide at Waverly Hills Sanatorium, during a thoracoplasty procedure "they would cut you from the base of your neck, all the way down your back, around both sides of you, open you up like a door, and saw out up to seven ribs." The idea was to collapse part of the lung in order to give it a chance to heal, and this would frequently require multiple surgeries at a time when medical practices were far less humane than they are today.

Even if patients survived the surgeries they were frequently left unable to stand upright.

With much more medical research and knowledge behind us, it's easy for us to look back now and shake our heads in wonder. But the medical professionals at the time were applying treatments based on their existing knowledge and understanding. We look back on these medical histories from the shoulders of the giants we stand on.

HAUNTED HOSPITALS, ASYLUMS, AND PSYCHIATRIC INSTITUTIONS

CANADA

ALBERTA

Charles Camsell Hospital: We Don't Want to Be Here

Edmonton

Jocelyn Chisaakay and her best friend, Tara, were walking through the Inglewood neighbourhood of Edmonton, Alberta. Snow covered the ground, reflecting the blue light from the street lights and squeaking beneath their boots. It was late and they were cold and unhappy.

"Look," Tara said, nudging Jocelyn with her elbow. "It's that old haunted hospital. We should take a look!"

"No, no, we shouldn't," Jocelyn replied, and her heart began to pound in her chest. "Let's just go."

"C'mon! We're right here. Just one look."

Jocelyn shook her head, gripped by a fear she'd never felt before, and refused to even *look* at the abandoned hospital. Even as Tara tugged her across the street toward it, Jocelyn kept her head down, watching her boots crush the snow beneath them through a cloud of her own condensed breath. She was repelled by the empty building as much as Tara seemed to be drawn to it. "I don't like this," she said. "I'm scared. Can we just go?"

Just as they reached the thin strand of trees that edged the hospital property, a long, scary howl cut through the night. It originated from the hospital and went on and on — it sounded fierce, but Jocelyn had the definite impression that whatever was making it was in pain.

Even once the howl had faded away, it echoed in Jocelyn's mind, and she didn't dare raise her voice above a whisper. "Did you hear that?"

"I heard it," Tara whispered back.

The girls left that area as quickly as they could — even Tara's curiosity about the haunted hospital had abated — but the howl haunted Jocelyn. Who or what had made it? What did it mean? Why had she been so afraid to even look at the hospital? What would she have seen if she had? Whatever it was, she prayed it might rest easy.

Years later she moved back to her reservation and shared the story of her encounter at the Charles Camsell Hospital with her father. He said that her grandfather, who had been a healer in life, had passed away in that hospital from cancer. Perhaps, suggested her father, he just wanted to say hello.

Why had Jocelyn been afraid to even look at the hospital? What would she have seen if she had?

Jocelyn thought perhaps he was right, but if it were her grandfather, why did he sound so menacing?

"It was intense," Jocelyn said when relaying the story to us. "To this day there are times I wish we'd gone back...."

History of the Charles Camsell Hospital

The original building that eventually became the Charles Camsell Hospital was constructed in 1913 by Jesuits, and it was used as a Jesuit college for boys until 1942. At the beginning of the Second World War, the American army took over the property as part of its "friendly invasion" of Canada. Several new buildings were constructed, and the resulting facility was used to house and support the American army personnel and engineers constructing the Alaska Highway.

When the highway was finished in 1944, the Canadian government took over the site and turned it into the Edmonton Military Hospital, meant to treat injured soldiers returning from war abroad. Several of the buildings constructed by the American army had been connected to the main building by a series of tunnels and corridors.

Next the government converted it from a military hospital to a tuberculosis hospital to serve the Inuit and First Nations groups in Alberta, Yukon Territory, and part of the Northwest Territories. The Royal Canadian Army Medical Corps and Indian Health Services ran the facility together for several months, and then on June 1, 1946, the land and buildings were officially transferred from the Canadian Department of Defence to the Department of National Health and Welfare. A couple months later, on August 26, 1946, the Charles Camsell Hospital officially opened as an "Indian sanatorium."

But buildings, like people, eventually wear out, and in 1964 the government began construction of a new hospital building on the property. In July 1967 it became the functional hospital, and the old Jesuit college building was torn down. That new building is the one that stands on the property today.

During its time as an Indian hospital, the Charles Camsell was largely used to treat tuberculosis patients. Government-assembled teams would travel to remote indigenous communities to test people for tuberculosis (TB) and, if anyone showed signs of the disease, transport them back to the hospital for treatment.

Because tuberculosis does not discriminate in choosing its victims, patients ranged in age from the very young to the very old, and every age in between. Those afflicted were taken away from their families and flown to a hospital far from home, and a large number of those patients did not leave the hospital alive. Sadly, many of those who died at the Camsell never even had their bodies returned to their loved ones, leaving families with unanswered questions and without closure. Rumours of bodies buried on the grounds persist to this day, in part because the bodies of people who died weren't returned to their communities. In fact, the current property owners hired an Albertan historian, Michael Payne, to research the probability of it being a burial site. He found no evidence to support the idea, but that doesn't stop people from wondering and speculating.

By the 1970s there was no longer a need for a dedicated tuberculosis hospital in Alberta, so the Camsell's function shifted to that of a general treatment hospital, and it functioned as such until 1992 when it closed down. The Charles Camsell Hospital was officially decommissioned in 1993.

The old hospital facility is currently owned by Edmonton developer Gene Dub, who has undertaken the long and expensive process of removing the asbestos from the building, with the goal of converting it into apartments and condos.

No doubt the long time that it has spent empty has fuelled the stories of ghosts and spirits lingering around the property, along with the rumours of booby traps and barbed wire–wrapped railings meant to discourage vandals and squatters. But given its emotion-filled history one has to imagine these details are only gasoline on the fire.

Of the reported hauntings at the hospital, Edmonton historian Danielle Metcalfe-Chenail says, "Some have said they've seen figures in the windows or have broken in and had weird things happen to them.... There's a lot of people I've talked to that think their ancestor's spirits haven't found peace and they're still wandering. For a lot of people, it was not a happy place."

Daytime Investigation

Intrigued by the rumours and stories surrounding the Charles Camsell Hospital, paranormal investigators Rona Anderson and Ben Myckan, decided to investigate it for themselves. They suspected they would find something because, as Ben said in an interview, "When you yank somebody out of their community, and everything they know … I think there's anger, there's fear, frustration, desperation — all this stuff." Add that to the typical high emotions associated with a hospital stay, and it's a recipe for a whole lot of residual emotional energy … and maybe something more than that, too.

Rona and Ben weren't "100 percent sanctioned" (as they put it) to enter the Camsell Hospital, but they made friends with the security guard and he let them in. An outbuilding on the west end of the property connected to the main building through an underground tunnel, so rather than going in the locked front doors, they entered underground. Can you think of a better way to begin a paranormal investigation than by climbing through an underground tunnel?

After its closure the Charles Camsell Hospital was used as a set for a couple of movies. Because Dave Thomas's *Whitecoats* and *Ginger Snaps II: Unleashed* were filmed there, walking through the old hospital was a surreal experience. Some parts of it were empty and neglected while others appeared to be still in use and fully functional.

One of Rona and Ben's first stops was an old operating room. The few things in the room included a metal shelf and a light panel that doctors used to view X-rays. When they looked at the light panel through their infrared camera, it was glowing. There was no reason for a glow because it wasn't turned on, but it was luminous. Ben isn't sure this was paranormal — it could be ascribed to an electrical short or even just an old bulb acting abnormally, as they sometimes do — but the light was pulsing.

Intrigued by the light panel, Rona and Ben turned on an audio recorder and placed it on the metal shelf in the room. "We left it and left the floor," Rona said. "Like, literally, there was nobody on that floor, it was just us in the building — we could not hear mice or anything." Later when they played the recording back, however, they could hear all sorts of things on it: the sound of movement, and a loud bang, like someone slamming a hand down on the shelf. This was especially interesting since when they came back to retrieve their recorder, it had been moved from its original position, almost as though someone had hit the shelf and knocked it over. They could also hear an authoritative male voice calling, "Karen! Karen!" They interpreted that as perhaps a doctor calling a nurse. The recorder also captured the sound of metal tools being shifted on a tray and clanking against one another, but on Rona and Ben's visit, there were no tools in the room at all.

Given the evidence they'd just collected, the two were convinced there was something going on at the hospital. They made plans to return for an overnight vigil, but on this trip they didn't come alone, bringing a whole team of paranormal investigators and even a film crew. The plan was to record as much as possible and make a documentary out of it.

Nighttime Vigil

Some people take paranormal investigations very seriously. Some do not. The beginning of Rona and Ben's investigation demonstrates that perfectly. Before the group entered the hospital, through the front door this time, Rona gathered them all together to perform a protection ceremony, a precaution that those in her group believed was important and necessary. While she was doing it, the security guard who was letting them in (for the low, low price of a bottle of "the good stuff") wandered over. He stood in the middle of the group scratching his butt. Then without warning he snorted, horked up a huge phlegm ball, and spat it out.

That was when Rona decided, "Okay, I guess we're done with that."

Inside the Camsell, the party split up into several smaller groups. Rona and Ben were together in one of those groups, and they decided to begin their exploration in the basement, where the morgue was located.

To reach the basement they took an elevator. There were actually two elevators side by side, but only one of them was functional; the other didn't even have power.

The morgue was interesting. There was still equipment left behind that they could check out, but on that particular night the real action didn't happen in the morgue — it happened back out in the hallway with the elevators. While they were in the morgue, the little group heard the "ding" of an elevator and the sound of its doors opening. When they looked to see who was joining them, it was the non-operational elevator, the one that didn't even have power to it. Its doors had opened.

Intrigued, they approached, intending to enter the elevator to see what was going on, but as they neared the doors, they closed again and the elevator started to ascend. It started to ascend — with no power and no passenger! At least, none that anyone could see.

"Where would we have ended up if we'd gotten in?" Ben wondered aloud, relaying the story.

At another point in their visit, when one of their groups was on the fourth floor, they heard really loud footsteps above them. At first they thought it might just be one of their party walking on the floor above them, but then they realized that normal everyday footsteps simply don't carry that clearly from the floor above.

Another area of the hospital where they expected paranormal activity was the former psych ward, so that was their next destination. It did not disappoint, though everyone had a different experience. In particular, Rona had a profound experience because, as she says, "I can see spirits who haven't crossed over.... I can't, unfortunately, say I see your grandma and this is what your grandma says. I see the things who haven't crossed over and a lot of them aren't very pretty and a lot of them are angry or they are trying to be frightening...." Not everyone in their group claims psychic abilities of any kind, but even so they all had a chilling experience in this part of the hospital.

In the old psych ward there were office areas separated from the main ward by Plexiglas windows. As they wandered through this area, someone in their group noticed something he thought was new and asked, "Were those handprints there before?" When they looked, everyone could clearly see handprints streaking down the window. It looked as though someone had banged open palms against the glass and pulled them down the length of the pane.

Unfortunately, no one could remember if the handprints had been there when they first arrived on the floor or not, but it was a disconcerting experience that put several members of the team on edge.

It was around this time in the visit that some of the investigators could smell unexplained pipe or cigar smoke. Ben says, "We were kinda arguing about if it was pipe or cigar, but cigars smell nasty whereas pipes are more pleasant.... I smelled cigar, but some said it was a pipe."

It was also on that floor that Rona saw the first visible manifestation she encountered on this investigation, a fifteen-year-old girl with "an incredible amount of emotional pain." Although the girl was dressed in a hospital gown, Rona's impression was that she was from the late 1970s. She was a Caucasian girl whose long brown hair occasionally obscured her face as she moved and hung her head. Her wrists were wrapped because she'd tried unsuccessfully to commit suicide and she was twitchy and scratching herself, creating deep welts, "almost like a meth addict, but she wasn't a meth addict."

"When are Mom and Dad coming to pick me up?" she said. Over and over. All she wanted was for her parents to come and get her, to take her away from this place. At first she seemed to think the little group of investigators could help her, and she hung around for a bit, shaking and scratching and asking when her parents were coming to get her. Eventually, presumably when she realized that only Rona could see her and that no one there had the power to help her at that time, she faded off.

Rona couldn't say if the girl had died at the hospital or if she'd died elsewhere but felt that her place was at the Charles Camsell. Either way it seems pretty clear that she didn't want to be there any longer, and yet she was unable to move on.

Many of the team of investigators, even those who could not see the girl, were uncomfortable on that floor and wanted to leave it. In fact, most of them did go elsewhere, leaving only a trio of people in the psych ward.

The investigators then split into three groups: the first remained on the psych ward, and two others went elsewhere. Rona was in the second group, and Ben was with his friend Darin in the third.

That's when the walkie-talkies started to act up.

Suddenly, everyone in the various investigative groups heard an unearthly scream of pain or horror come through the walkie-talkies.

Before they could process the ramifications of the sound, or try to ascertain its source, Darin's voice came on the line. "Leslie, are you there? Leslie? Are you okay? Leslie, are you there?" he asked.

Leslie was the name of his girlfriend at the time, so it might not seem unreasonable that he would want to make sure she was all right ... except for three things. First, Leslie wasn't on the grounds of the hospital — she wasn't even in the country. She was away on a humanitarian mission as a nurse in Africa. Second, some people heard his voice come over the walkie-talkies while others heard only silence. And third, Darin didn't have a walkie-talkie. In his group Ben was carrying the handset.

"They will mimic you," Rona explained, speaking of the spirits who linger in such places. If it really was a spirit mimicking Darin's voice, that begs the questions — what purpose was it trying to achieve? And how did it know what name to use?

Everyone was pretty unnerved by then, but as Rona repeatedly said during our interview, there's no point in doing investigations if you're not willing to face that fear and keep looking. It makes no sense to go seeking paranormal activity and then run away screaming at the first sign of it that you encounter, so the intrepid group kept on.

On the pediatric floor of the hospital, one of the groups tried an experiment. They cut open a large garbage bag so that it was a big square of dark plastic. Laying that out on the ground, they covered it in baby powder and placed a small ball, the kind a child would play with, in the middle of the powder-covered plastic sheet. The idea was that if anything disturbed the ball, tracks or marks would be left in the powder. Then they set up an infrared camera to record the ball, got on the elevator, and left the floor to whatever spirits might be there.

Later when they played back the recording, they were blown away. Rona says, "You heard the elevator doors close, and as soon as those elevator doors closed, it [the floor] came alive. You could hear somebody pushing a medical cart, you could hear the beep, beep, beep of a heart machine ... you could hear all this stuff just like the [whole floor] was operating again."

The only movement captured on video was a moment when something unseen struck the camera and moved it slightly off to the left.

Imagine how disorienting it must have been to be watching one reality and hearing another! Completely surreal.

Unfortunately, the video was accidentally recorded over, so we were unable to watch it, but Rona and several others saw it before it was lost, so we were able to recount here what they witnessed. The team was distressed to discover that their incredible video had been lost, however, sacrificed to the recording of a television sitcom.

When Rona's group investigated the basement, they discovered an auditorium they assumed had been used for physical therapy and patient recreation. It had basketball hoops, two projection booths, and various other bits of equipment. "When I went down there," Rona said, there were "a whole bunch of Aboriginal spirits. And they were feeling everything between angry, sad, despair — every emotion possible except anything positive."

One spirit in particular drew her attention: an Aboriginal elder. When Rona saw him, he was sitting on a bench against the wall, holding his head in his hands. She approached and spoke to him, and he looked at her with eyes that were wells of sadness and said, "We did not ask to be here.... We don't want to be here anymore."

Rona got the impression that there were a lot of spirits, Indigenous and otherwise, on the grounds of the Charles Camsell Hospital. She recalled, "I found, going through all the floors, that there were spirits there, but they were reluctant spirits, and a lot of them didn't want to come out." But Rona believes they are trapped there in the hospital. Rona and Ben want to go back sometime and release them all. "They're waiting. They're waiting for someone to come get them."

As the night wore on, the team grew mentally and physically exhausted, but Rona and an investigator named Stephanie decided to visit the first floor. Rona had sensed bad emanations coming from one of the offices down the hallway from the main entrance, and the two of them went inside to check it out. "I wasn't scared," Rona says, "but I could feel this deep, negative — I don't even want to say 'evil' because we don't believe in demons, and we don't believe in devils … it's all human, it's all negative humans that cause a lot of this stuff — so I guess what I would say is the person who either occupied that office when they were alive, or decided to occupy it after they were dead, was a really nasty, nasty person." Rona felt sick to her stomach in the room and decided not to linger inside.

Before leaving the hospital, Rona and Ben had a celebratory shot of Crown Royal with the security guard. Then, while Ben took Stephanie home, Darin drove Rona back to his place. When they got there, he offered her a drink, which she accepted. After drinking it she went to the bathroom. That's the last thing she remembers from that night.

When Ben arrived some time later, Darin said, "I'm really worried about Rona. She's been in the bathroom a long time."

Ben opened the door and found her asleep on the floor, scratching at her arms like the girl she'd seen in the psych ward of the hospital. Ben and Darin were unable to wake her up and could do nothing but wrap a blanket around her and wait until she woke of her own accord — this was something that had never happened to her before.

In fact, no one who was involved with the investigation was unaffected. The next day they were all fatigued to a degree that couldn't be explained by mere sleep deprivation, and many had disturbing nightmares for weeks afterward.

"I'm not super affected by investigations or stuff like that," says Ben. "But every single person that was there felt physically and emotionally drained."

Rona thinks the combination of drinking alcohol and not protecting herself spiritually before, or immediately after, leaving the building is what caused the problem. "When you drink alcohol or do drugs of any kind," she says, "you open yourself up to things."

Had Rona been a way out for the girl from the psychiatric ward?

"See, half the time in these investigations, you end up with more questions than answers," said Ben, and we're inclined to believe him.

If there are spirits trapped there at the Camsell, the news is not all grim, however. Current owner and developer Gene Dub recently spoke at a full-day symposium about the hospital, indicating that once the site is completely safe from asbestos (they are just finishing up a huge effort to remove it all from the building), he will welcome Aboriginal elders to perform a healing ceremony at the property. It is a step toward

The former Charles Camsell Hospital has been undergoing the long and expensive process of removing asbestos from the building so that it can be converted into condominium apartments.

reconciliation with Canada's Indigenous people, and it could help begin the process of healing for those still with us, as well as for spirits who don't want to be here anymore.

Edmonton General Hospital: Three Hauntings

Edmonton

The Edmonton General Hospital opened its doors in 1895, and it still functions as a continuing care centre.

According to the Paranormal Scene Investigation Canada website, there are three main hauntings associated with this hospital.

The first occurs on the eighth floor in the area of the hospital that was once pediatrics — Ward 8B. There, people have claimed to hear the sounds of crying children even though there are no children anywhere in the ward.

The second haunting also occurs, at least in part, on the eighth floor. It is said that the full-bodied apparition of a woman has been seen wandering over the sixth and the eighth floors. Legend says this is the ghost of a mother who is now spending eternity in search of her lost child.

The third and final ghost is reported to be that of an electrician who was killed in an accident while working in the hospital basement. The stories say his ghost can still be spotted from time to time, lingering in the area where he passed away.

Pembina Hall: Love Beyond the Grave

Edmonton

Pembina Hall is a residential building for students on the University of Alberta campus, but for some time it functioned as a hospital and is, as a result, reported to be haunted. Built in 1914, it served as a residence for students but also contained classrooms, offices, and the anatomy department, the latter of which earned the building the nickname "the morgue." Pembina Hall's nickname was soon to become even more apt.

Pembina Hall, which served as a hospital and student residence, also housed for a time the anatomy department of the University of Alberta. The building is allegedly haunted.

At the end of the First World War an outbreak of Spanish influenza swept across the planet, killing more people than the Great War had. It is estimated that from 1918 to 1919 over 20 million people died from this pandemic, and some estimates range as high as 50 million or more, making it the worst pandemic in history. Canada was not immune: if you visit an old graveyard, you'll find a disproportionately high number of tombstones listing 1918 or 1919 as the year of death.

Throughout this global outbreak people were getting sick and dying so quickly that hospitals couldn't contain them all, and adaptable buildings were frequently commandeered for use as temporary hospitals. Pembina Hall was one of these. During its time as a hospital at least seventy-two people died at Pembina Hall. Because Pembina was intended as a place to live, rather than a place to die, it lacked the appropriate facilities to deal with the resulting corpses. In an attempt to prevent the spread of the disease through contact, the bodies were stored in the building's basement. Unfortunately, in the hot summertime the basement was a sweltering place, and as a result the bodies down there decomposed at an accelerated rate. With ventilation being what it was in the early 1900s, it is likely the odour of the rotting corpses would have been noticeable throughout the building. In fact, it is said that in Pembina Hall even today, nearly a hundred years later, on a hot summer day you can still catch a whiff of the foul smell of decomposition.

Another slightly less visceral story about Pembina Hall's time as a hospital involves a young couple. According to the University of Alberta student union's Spooky Places on Campus web page, the couple met and fell in love while they were attending the university. Then came the war, which tore them apart. He joined the army and went to fight for his country, and she stayed in Edmonton and volunteered as a nurse. She was working in Pembina Hall when she found a familiar face under her care — her beloved was back from the war but fighting a much more insidious foe than the Germans. She stayed by his side, trying to defeat the Spanish influenza, but to no avail. The stories say he died shortly after being reunited with her.

Spanish influenza was an especially horrific way to die. It was a long, lingering death, during which people often coughed so hard their eyes would bleed, and they would slowly suffocate, sometimes actually turning blue from lack of oxygen. Devastated by the incredibly traumatic loss of her love, the nurse ran to the nearby river valley and threw herself into the river. Her body was never recovered, but some people say that even now a ghostly couple — she in a nurse's uniform and he in army fatigues — can occasionally be spotted wandering hand in hand through the halls of Pembina.

Galt Hospital: A Vibrant Gathering Place for Spirits

Lethbridge

The Galt Museum and Archives, described as a vibrant gathering place designed to meet the historical, cultural, and educational needs of the community, resides in a building that was constructed in 1910 as part of the Galt Hospital. Belinda Crowson, an employee of the museum, has collected and written about eerie happenings at the museum over the years, and shared some intriguing details about the building with us while we were researching this book.

Many of the stories related to the building's historic use as a hospital involve a gentleman who died after falling down an elevator shaft on his way to surgery in 1933. The man, whom the staff call "George," is said to still linger in the building, and he makes his presence known by operating the elevator. The haunted elevator was recently replaced, but the old elevator would run between floors all on its own and sometimes even trap people alone inside for several hours at a time.

In addition to haunting the elevator, George is said to have made his presence felt in the basement. Incidents in the building have for so long been blamed on his ghost that staff have grown accustomed to shrugging off any strange happenings and saying, "It's just George."

One story Belinda shared from the days when the building was still a hospital was of a woman who came in to have a baby. At one point she was returning from the main floor lobby to her room on the top floor. She got on the elevator and pushed the button for the upper floor, but the elevator took her down to the basement instead.

When the elevator arrived in the basement, a man was standing on the other side of the doors looking at her. She didn't think anything about it until she realized that he was transparent — she could see right through him!

The woman frantically pushed buttons to close the door and return to the main lobby. When she emerged from the elevator, she hurried to the nurses' station and reported what had happened.

"Oh, that's just George," she was told. "He brings people downstairs when he's lonely."

Odd smells emanate from nowhere, and eerie sounds have been heard in otherwise empty corridors and rooms. Moving shadows and strange blue lights have also been reported by people in the museum.

One evening, after a researcher finished some work in the museum, he left, knowing he was the last person to exit the building. Once outside he felt compelled to look back up at the window of the room he had just left and locked up. In the window, smiling down and waving at him, were a little boy and girl.

Passersby on the street have also reported seeing a pair of children waving out the window long after the museum is closed and the building is locked up for the night. The children, nicknamed "Sarah" and "Alexander," are said to be associated with the old children's ward (known as the "Sunbeam Ward") of the Galt Hospital. Sarah appears to be somewhere between the ages of five and seven, and Alexander is between ten and twelve. The two are always seen together.

Belinda also reported that one of the previous custodians from the museum used to get frustrated when the lights in the rooms she was cleaning would randomly shut off all on their own. At other times, after she had left a room and turned off the lights, they would snap back on without anyone operating them. Believing the cause to be the ghosts of the playful young children, she would heave out a long sigh and then instruct the children to turn out the lights and go to bed. She said sometimes that worked, and the lights would go off as she had commanded.

Other staff have claimed to hear singing and animated discussions coming from empty rooms, but they can't be certain whether the singing is coming from the spirits of the playful children or are a side effect of an odd sound transfer occurring through the building's old bricks. And there's more than one report of staff members being disturbed from their work in an office by the sound of shuffling feet outside the door. When they get up to investigate the noise, no one is to be found in the hallway.

At one time in the building's history, Belinda shared, there was a tunnel attached to the morgue area of the building, an underground hallway that had been blocked off when the connecting building was torn down. This underground hallway now leads nowhere, but it is apparently a hot spot for paranormal activity, including reports of people being pushed, shoved, or touched while traversing it.

On one Halloween tour of the building, a high school student was accidentally left behind in that underground area. When the teacher returned to get her, the student claimed that some unseen presence had been "holding" her in the tunnel.

Another story that was shared with Belinda came from someone who had been a teenager in the 1960s. His story was about five young boys who snuck into the empty building after it was no longer in use as a hospital. While moving around the basement they were startled by the sound of footsteps heading in their direction. Frightened of being caught by a security guard, they fled. Once they were back outside, they looked up and saw a man standing in a second-floor window. He was dressed in a suit, wore a hat, and had a big red flower in his lapel. They were confused as to how the man in the window could have moved from the basement to the second floor so quickly, and they are now convinced that they had heard and seen one of the building's ghosts.

One final eerie tale from the building involved a telephone repairman who did some work there in 1979. For the first five years he worked there, he never experienced anything eerie or unexplained, but later on in his career he found himself alone in a dimly lit room in the back corner of the building, standing on a ladder. His partner — a man who went by the nickname "Grampa" — was upstairs. Grampa was supposed to feed down the wire they were installing.

While he waited for Grampa to push the wire down the pipe, he felt a tingling sensation on the back of his neck and a sudden draft of cold that made his toes go numb.

Getting down off the ladder, flashlight in hand, the repairman looked around, wondering if the draft had come from Grampa opening a nearby door. But there was nobody else around, inside or outside the room.

The man climbed back up on the ladder, where he felt a second draft of cold air blow into the room. Assuming his colleague was playing a trick on him from the corridor, he said, "Quit your fooling around, Grampa!"

Grampa's voice, muffled from his location upstairs, echoed down through the pipe. "I'm not fooling around. Just put the wire on the fish stick!"

The man immediately fled the basement room. His face was white with terror while he explained what had happened to both the secretary and Grampa.

Grampa laughed at what he said was the man's overactive imagination, but the man refused to ever return to the basement of the old Galt Hospital by himself.

Alberta Hospital for the Insane: A Woman Possessed

Ponoka

Known under many different names, including Alberta Mental Hospital, Ponoka Mental Hospital, and Alberta Hospital Building No. 1, the hospital in Ponoka, Alberta, was founded in 1911 and became the province's primary health-care facility and Alberta's first mental hospital.

The building still stands, transformed into the Centennial Centre for Mental Health and Brain Injury, and is now a nationally renowned psychiatric and brain-care facility. But for at least a few former employees of the Ponoka Mental Hospital, it will forever be the cause of endless nightmares.

The following story was first revealed to co-author Mark Leslie during a live radio show (*Coast to Coast AM with George Noory*) in March 2015. Leslie later interviewed the caller to get more details about the incredibly eerie experience.

The caller was a former staff member, whom we'll call "Pat" (and refer to as "he" though Pat's real name and gender is something we'd rather keep private). Pat worked at the psychiatric hospital for several decades. He relayed a story he had not previously shared — mostly because it was so horrifying he didn't want to think about it.

The story Pat shared concerns a woman we'll call "Martha Sutherland," who died sometime in the late 1980s or early 1990s. Martha had been admitted to the hospital as an adolescent around 1950, and she spent most of her formative years and all of her adult life in the hospital. "That was not uncommon," Pat said.

"Martha was in her mid-fifties in 1983 when the events in question happened." Pat went on to describe the conditions at Lawn Crest One, the unit where he worked. He conjured the old idea of the inmates running the asylum, a reference to the 1920 cult film *The Cabinet of Dr. Caligari*. "It was like that," he said. "That expression was literally true. The unit was out of control. It was horrible."

At the time Pat was working permanent night flow, and he said there were normally two or three staff members on duty for that shift. But because the unit was so difficult to control, it wasn't uncommon to have six staff members booked in. This was unusual at a time when it was almost unheard of for even four staff members to be on duty simultaneously in the same unit.

Pat described an all-staff meeting that included doctors, nurses, support workers, and all others, each there to discuss and share issues and decide upon solutions. They discussed the potential need for danger pay, as well as the possibility of bringing in tasers for the safety of the staff. And then, amid all of the discussion of violence and patient unruliness that had been causing these concerns, the topic of Martha Sutherland came up.

Someone immediately mentioned the possibility that Martha might be possessed, and several other staff members who regularly dealt with her kicking, punching, screaming, and biting immediately agreed. The issue was taken very seriously, and several rounds of discussion began. According to one of the workers who had access to the documents, in a single month at the hospital Martha had caused more staff injuries than there were in all other hospital incidents combined.

"There was talk about actually bringing in an exorcist in order to deal with her," recalled Pat.

Martha's room was adjacent to the television room where, when they were not on active duty or doing rounds, staff would relax and watch television or movies. That room had a direct connection, by ventilation shaft, to Martha's room.

"Sometimes when we were sitting there we'd hear voices that weren't coming from the television," Pat said. "You would hear voices as if she were talking to a second person, but when you went and checked in on her — right next door, so it was just a few steps away — she was lying there fast asleep and all by herself."

Pat also claimed that Martha's room was sometimes like being in an icebox. She would complain about the cold, and staff would move her to another warmer room, but within minutes of moving her, the room she'd been in would return to a normal temperature and the room she'd been moved to would turn ice cold.

"That was odd. But the worst …" Pat began in a shaky voice before several long seconds of silence. When Pat finally spoke again, almost half a minute later, his voice was a soft and gentle echo of its previously deep tones. "The worst was what happened one night in the seclusion room."

There was another long pause before Pat continued. "Sometimes, when patients lost control, we would have to put them in a private seclusion room so that they wouldn't hurt the staff or other patients." The seclusion room, as Pat described it, was a ten-by-twelve-foot room with a door at the front and a window at the back. The windowsill was sloped at a 45-degree angle to prevent anyone from being able to perch on it, and there was a large curtain on the inside of the room, meant to prevent too much stimulation from light and noise outside the room. Inside the room was a mattress, and there was a blanket known as a "strong sheet," made from multiple layers of canvas and designed to be difficult to tear.

"This one night," Pat said, "there were only three of us working on the night shift. Martha was yelling, hitting, punching, and kicking at us after coming out of her room screaming bloody murder." They weren't sure if it was a dream or a hallucination, but she would not be calmed down, and they had to tranquilize her and place her in a seclusion room.

Later on, in the wee hours of the morning, Pat was doing rounds to check on all of the patients. Something shocking awaited him in Martha's room.

"I walked in, pulled back the curtain, and turned on the night light in her room. Except she wasn't laying on the mattress. And she wasn't standing in a corner some place, which patients sometimes did.

"Looking to the right I saw something that I'll never get out of my head," Pat said. "Martha was literally standing at about my shoulder height on the side of the wall, facing out into the room. She looked just like somebody who was standing on the floor and looking straight ahead; but because she was horizontal, not vertical, she was facing down and staring straight at the floor.

"Her nightgown was done up around her, and parts of it were hanging down as if gravity still worked properly on it; even though gravity didn't seem to be working on her body in the same way. Her hair was shorter, a closely cut perm style, so it wasn't long enough to be hanging down. But there she stood, still and unmoving."

Martha didn't acknowledge Pat in any way. He couldn't tell if she was awake or asleep, and he didn't stick around long enough to find out. "I took one look at her, realized what I was seeing, then I turned around, walked straight out, and returned to the TV room.

"I never told any of my colleagues about what I had seen. When I returned to the television room, and the supervisor asked how everything was, I just said, 'Yep. Everything was fine,' and spent the rest of my time trying desperately to block that image from my mind."

Until the night Pat called in to that *Coast to Coast AM* radio program to share the story, he had never breathed a word of the tale to anyone. And a week after that show, prior to a scheduled call to share the story with Mark in more detail, Pat met with a former colleague from the hospital, someone who knew Martha. Pat told his former co-worker the story and watched as a really strange look came over his colleague's face. And when Pat finished, the other man shared something that he, too, had never breathed a word of to anybody, mostly because he had believed what he had seen to be an optical illusion.

Pat's colleague had been working the day shift and had checked in on Martha's room. She stared straight ahead, not acknowledging him at all, but he could have sworn that her feet were about two inches above the floor. He had, at the time, shaken his head and dismissed it as the work of an overtired mind or perhaps a trick of the light, but when he heard Pat's story, he wondered if perhaps he hadn't been mistaken after all.

Pat felt good to be able to finally share the tale but the experience still has a deep haunting effect. "The hairs on my head are standing up, and it has been well over thirty years since it happened," Pat said. "I don't go to horror movies anymore. I made the mistake of watching the original version of the movie *Carrie*. Scenes from movies like that remind me too much about Martha and what I saw that night."

BRITISH COLUMBIA

Riverview Hospital: A Very Scary Place

Coquitlam

"Riverview was a very scary place," Teresa Balfour told Matt Meuse of the *Globe and Mail* in a 2014 interview. "You didn't know if you'd ever get out."

Balfour was referring to some of the horrific therapies that were once common practice for treatment of mental illness, thinking specifically of her brother's death at the East Lawn facility in 1990. But the grounds and buildings of Riverview, which have been a popular filming location for such notable eerie television programs as *The X-Files*, *Fringe*, and *Supernatural*, have hosted almost as many creepy and interesting tales as have been explored on those shows.

Phenomena that have been reported at this site include shadowy apparitions believed to be former patients, mysterious ghostly stirrings and echoes in the abandoned underground tunnels that connect the buildings, phantom footsteps, inexplicable moving objects, slamming doors and windows, and disembodied voices telling visitors to "go home" and "leave us alone."

Riverview has been a popular filming location for such TV programs as The X-Files, Fringe, *and* Supernatural.

Riverview Hospital operated as a mental health facility between 1913 and 2012. The West Lawn building was originally constructed to hold a maximum of 480 patients, but ended up housing 1,919 occupants. By 1956 the hospital had reached more than 4,300 patients. Former staff reminisced about carrying ice-cream pails full of pills up to patients, and told stories of bed crowding — they were so tightly packed together that a bed had to be pushed out of the room in order to be made, after which it would be pushed back in and the next one would be hauled out, repeating the process.

Over the years, reductions occurred and different facilities were closed, including West Lawn in 1983 and the Crease Clinic in 1992. By 2002 there were a mere eight hundred beds in all of Riverview, and in 2005 the East Lawn building was closed. The North Lawn building closed in 2007, and in 2012, just a few years after it was added to the Canadian Register of Historic Places, Riverview Hospital closed down completely.

Connolly Lodge, Cottonwood Lodge, and a high-security facility for the mentally ill are still in operation on the grounds, and in December 2015 the provincial government announced a $175 million investment that would rebuild and re-establish the grounds as a centre for mental health treatment, which will reinvigorate the population on the grounds. Construction is scheduled to begin in 2017 with the opening designated for 2019. But in the meantime, there are enough lingering spirits and eerie tales reported in this location to keep even the most avid ghost researcher busy for years.

As mentioned, parts of the Riverview Hospital have been popular for filming movies and television, and the location has been referred to as one of the most filmed sites in all of Canada. But while these fictional films and television shows are being shot on location, not all of the eerie chills and terrors experienced by the actors come from the scripts.

An actor known as Caz, whose story appears in Joel A. Sutherland's book *Haunted Canada 4*, got far more than he expected when he spent the night in the West Lawn building and the Crease Clinic.

In 2004 Caz had a small part in a horror film. When he wasn't needed on set, he took some time to explore various parts of the building, and he described getting bad feelings in multiple locations in the building, as well as two startling visual encounters.

Caz said that two out of the five floors of the West Lawn building left him with strong negative vibes. In the basement tunnels, in particular, he experienced an uncanny and overwhelming bad feeling. But it was the repeated encounter with a spectral canine that left the deepest impression on him.

Over the course of the six days he spent in the building, he would explore the dark hallway of the fourth floor, usually between midnight and 2 a.m. From the far end of the dark corridor, lit only by the red glow of the EXIT sign at the far end, Caz saw something moving toward him. It was low to the ground and it moved quickly — a dark shape that appeared to be a dog.

Charging toward him, impossibly noiseless, the creature seemed to be attacking. As it grew closer, Caz could see that the dog appeared partially transparent. And it always disappeared just before reaching him.

"I didn't believe it at first," Caz said, "until I saw it three separate nights in the same corridor."

Intrigued by the feelings and sights, Caz patrolled the building with a camera and took a picture of what had been described to him by the building's liaison as the "Candy Lady Ghost."

The Candy Lady Ghost is believed to reside in and near a fourth-floor room called the "Ladybug Room." This room is unique for two reasons: While the door doesn't have a doorknob, it's the only room in the entire building that appears to have ambient light coming from somewhere inside, visible from the crack at the bottom of the door. And the door is locked tight. As hard as Caz tried to pry the door open at the time, it simply would not budge.

When he knelt down and tried to peer inside the room, he couldn't see much, but he could have sworn he could hear someone, or something, breathing on the other side of the door.

As a self-declared non-believer in ghosts prior to filming at Riverview Hospital, Caz left the building as a firm believer.

In a 2014 *Huffington Post* article, a janitor who worked at the hospital after it closed down described his job there as the scariest thing he had ever done in his life. He portrayed the underground tunnels as creepy, a place where he constantly heard echoes behind him. Each time he had to move through them, he never dared to look back over his shoulder, rushing to get out of them as quickly as possible. He also mentioned hearing snickering, laughter, and whispers coming from behind the closed doors of what used to be the patients' rooms whenever he walked the long corridors by himself.

Scott and Shelby Leroy, who head up 6 Feet Under (6feetunder. ca), a non-profit group dedicated to professional, respectful paranormal investigations, conducted investigations using electronic recording devices in the West Lawn, Centre Lawn, and East Lawn buildings at multiple times in 2014 and 2015. Using digital recorders and a Spirit Box, which is a device that uses a modified AM/FM radio to scan frequencies at a high rate of speed and captures EVP (electrical voice phenomena), the group recorded multiple inexplicable voices and noises.

Captured in recordings on the group's website, you can listen to the sounds of children screaming. They are ghostly voices that seem to mock the words of the investigators, repeating words such as "yeah" and "perfect." There are also feminine voices saying "help me" and "don't go," and calling out for "Matt," one of the team's investigators.

Some of the other recordings from that website include the sound of spirits singing and giggling. More aggressive voices are verbally abusive to the investigators and utter "get out" and more blatant threats, such as "just die!" Some of the spirits are heard to say, "We're locking you out!" when a tour guide leading the group had trouble unlocking a door in the attic. Still others offered friendly advice: one feminine voice repeatedly warns Scott, saying, "Run, Scott!"

As stated on their website and reported in a 2014 Calgary *Metro* article, the Leroys conduct their investigations as professionals and avoid sacred spaces such as cemeteries. "We're not there to cause disrespect whatsoever," Scott Leroy says. "We are there to gather more information about the paranormal and to find out unknown things from spirits."

But, unlike the Leroys, not all ghost hunters behave with professionalism and respect.

Heather Anderson, a caregiver who worked at the operational section of Riverview Hospital, feeding, bathing, and looking after the needs of patients, posted a cautionary article on the PSICAN (Paranormal Studies and Inquiry Canada) website regarding the invasion of privacy. She described ghost hunters who would occasionally appear at all hours of the night, showing little consideration for patients, their families, and staff. While she admitted to having experienced strange events while working at Riverview, including a voice close to her ear saying "Don't do that" when she was standing alone in one of the bedrooms, she expressed a desire for those intrigued to respect and consider the privacy of not only current residents, but also those who once lived and perhaps died there.

Vancouver General Hospital: The Phantom of Room 415

Vancouver

Nurses are expected to be calm, cool, and collected in the face of utmost tragedy, and in life-and-death situations. But despite their training and experience, they can sometimes find the passing of a patient difficult to accept. And sometimes a patient displays an uncanny will to live, to survive a tragedy, and might not fully accept passing on to the next world. Such was the case in this tale of room 415 in the burn unit of Vancouver General Hospital.

In October of 1975 a series of giant explosions rocked a towering grain elevator on the waterfront of North Vancouver. Multiple blasts set off an unrelenting blaze that, according to a *Wilmington Morning Star* article, took over ninety minutes for firemen to bring under control, forced hundreds of nearby residents to flee their homes, and injured sixteen workmen, four of whom died and one whose body was never found.

"There was a sharp explosion that must have shaken loose a lot of [grain] dust, and then came the big one — a great roar that went through the building," said Barney Chapman, an electrician who witnessed the explosions. "I saw one man just outside who'd had his clothes ripped right off. The others came staggering out of the building and even though I knew them, I couldn't recognize some of them because of the dirt and burns."

The blast and fire was blamed on conveyer belt friction. "It must have generated a spark or fire that detonated grain dust in the building," explained a survivor.

The tragedy that began at the complex, used for loading grain shipments bound overseas, continued in the nearby burn unit of the Vancouver General Hospital (VGH), as documented in Robert Belyk's book *Ghosts: True Tales of Eerie Encounters*.

One of the victims who arrived at VGH was a twenty-eight-year-old we'll call "Bryan." His prognosis was negative. He was in terrible shape, but staff at the hospital were surprised and delighted to learn that Bryan was a fighter and, though facing a tremendous challenge and unimaginable pain, he struggled against the odds and fought valiantly. In room 415, Bryan refused to give in to his injuries.

Though staff, friends, and family encouraged him in his battle against the impossible odds, Bryan eventually ran out of strength and could no longer fight. His heart finally gave out.

Just before he passed away, Bryan is said to have confided in a nurse that he was in too much pain and was very tired. His tough will and courage made it extremely difficult for the nurses to accept he had died.

Not long after his death, a nurse walked into room 415 and spotted something odd on the empty bed. The covers shifted, almost as if somebody lying in the bed had rolled over in his sleep. As she looked on, shocked, she could have sworn that she also heard something: the quiet, rhythmic sound of a man breathing in his sleep.

Before too long, other nurses and staff members reported seeing and hearing strange things both in and near the room, including blaring radios suddenly turning on, the toilet inexplicably flushing, and odd sensations of prickly cold.

On one occasion a male nurse, preoccupied with getting room 415 ready for the next patient, walked in and noticed a colleague's white form out of the corner of his eye. When he turned to ask what he thought was his colleague for assistance, the white form fell to the floor — nothing more than a pile of dressings. There was nobody there at all; the nurse suspected he had seen Bryan.

Apparently Bryan wasn't just visible to the staff of the hospital. As someone who could fully understand the plight of the burn victims in the unit, he appeared to some of the patients who spent time in room 415. A nurse recounted to Robert Belyk that Bryan had once appeared to a woman who, like Bryan, had been admitted to the hospital with burns so severe that it seemed unlikely she would live very long.

The woman described a strange young man who had visited her at a time when only close family members were allowed access. He had told her his name was Bryan and kept her company.

On another occasion, a patient in the adjacent room, room 413, remarked that a mysterious young male doctor had appeared in the middle of the night to help the patient deal with his extreme pain.

Despite the odd sightings, eerie occurrences, and inexplicable visits from a stranger that seemed to match young Bryan's description, staff members felt that the spiritual presence of Bryan in and around room 415 was not that of an evil spirit. Rather, the stories pointed at a young man who wanted to make sure that everybody knew he was still around and, in some ways, still fighting the good fight alongside them, hoping to make a positive difference.

EASTERN CANADA

Centracare Psychiatric Facility: Eerie Cries and Shadowy Figures

Saint John, New Brunswick

The building that was the Centracare Psychiatric Facility has long been demolished, replaced by a lush, privately owned but publicly accessible park, offering picturesque views of both the Saint John skyline and the eerily attractive Reversing Falls.

The Reversing Falls are a series of rapids on the Saint John River, so called because the flow of the semidiurnal tides and underwater ledges cause the flow of water to reverse against the prevailing current. But they aren't the only unique and seemingly supernatural thing at this location.

According to the now-defunct Haunted North America website, electronic devices cease to work consistently on the site of the old facility, eerie disembodied voices are heard, and mysterious mists and shadowy figures believed to be the ghostly apparitions of former patients and staff of the old facility are reported by visitors.

The site of Wolastoq Park (Wolastoq means "beautiful river") is maintained by J.D. Irving, Limited, and was once the location of the Centracare Psychiatric Facility. Founded in 1835, it was called the Provincial Lunatic Asylum until 1985, and it was the first mental health facility constructed in British North America. At one time it housed as many as 1,697 patients. In the late 1990s patients were moved to a new facility in nearby suburban South Bay. The old Centracare building was demolished in 1999.

According to a story on the PSICAN website, a security guard patrolling the grounds in 1991, when the building was still operational, met with the paranormal. As the guard passed the churchyard, he heard the distinct sound of a baby crying. He searched everywhere, bewildered by the sound. He wondered where it could be coming from because he didn't know which wards had children or toddlers, but no matter where he looked, he couldn't find the source of the crying.

When he radioed the front desk to report the anomaly, he was informed of two things: There hadn't been babies in the facility since 1937. And it wasn't uncommon for people to hear the disturbing sound of a baby's cry echoing eerily through the dark of night.

Victoria General Hospital: Take Me to the Other Side

Halifax, Nova Scotia

Halifax is a city known to have more than its fair share of ghosts, perhaps not just because of the age of the city (it was originally founded in 1749), but also because one of the greatest disasters in Canadian history occurred there. In December 1917 the French munitions ship the SS *Mont-Blanc* collided with the Norwegian ship the SS *Imo* in the narrows near Halifax Harbour, resulting in a massive explosion that killed close to two thousand people and injured nearly nine thousand others.

Some believe that a tragic event, like the Halifax Explosion, can result in the inability of countless lost souls to find their way to the other side and to peace. Others believe that some of those lost spirits are sympathetic to those who are suffering or in pain, and they behave as a sort of a spirit guide whose purpose is to help newly departed lost souls find their own eternal peace.

One of them might just be the "Old Grey Nun" from the Victoria General Hospital.

We first learned about this legend from Halifax author and storyteller Steve Vernon, who wrote about her in his 2009 book, *Halifax Haunts: Exploring the City's Spookiest Spaces*.

Established in 1887, the Victoria General Hospital, located at 1278 Tower Road, originally began as a city hospital in the 1850s.

In a chapter entitled "The Old Grey Nun," Vernon relays a story shared with him about a woman named Bonnie. Bonnie was still a relatively new nurse when she encountered the Old Grey Nun on one of her nightly rounds.

Walking quietly from room to room in the dark with her flashlight, Bonnie checked on each patient in turn before arriving at the room of an elderly gentleman by the name of Edgar. Bonnie was quite fond of Edgar — perhaps the sweet old man reminded her of her own father, who had already passed on. Because of this personal connection, and because she knew that Edgar's health was failing, she always looked forward to seeing him. But one particular night, when she approached his room with no light but that of her flashlight, she was surprised to find that Edgar wasn't alone.

The room, she said, was filled with a soft grey light that she described as similar to the early morning light that accompanies grey fog rising up from the sea. It was bright enough that Bonnie didn't need her flashlight to see the Old Grey Nun standing at Edgar's bedside, looking down at the sweet old man. The figure's lips moved noiselessly, as if she were praying under her breath.

Bonnie didn't disturb the two. She stood in the doorway and watched, overcome with the feeling, as she saw the Old Grey Nun lift her hand to Edgar's brow, that the nun might be saying goodbye to a dear old friend. As the feeling overtook her and she took a deep breath, it seemed to Bonnie as if a bright light had suddenly been turned on. She closed her eyes quickly, and when she opened them a moment later, the bright light, the dull grey light, and the Old Grey Nun were all gone. All that lingered in Edgar's room was the faint scent of incense.

It was obvious to Bonnie that Edgar had died. She reported that he had a peaceful look on his face, a soft smile, as if he had just shared a fine joke with a dear friend.

When Bonnie later shared her experience with the head nurse, the head nurse simply smiled and remarked that the Old Grey Nun had been spotted around the hospital for years. It was believed she might have been a nurse who worked there during the time of the Halifax Explosion.

Bonnie was convinced after that late-night sighting that she would likely see the Old Grey Nun at least one more time, perhaps, she reflected, one final time before going home.

Bonnie has since passed on. We wonder if she died with a smile on her lips similar to Edgar's, looking up at the soft grey light and the friendly face of a spirit who was there to guide her on her way to eternal rest.

ONTARIO

Hamilton Psychiatric Hospital:
Cries of the Insane at Century Manor

Hamilton

Century Manor, the last remaining building from the Hamilton Asylum for the Insane, is tucked behind the northeast side of the $581 million St. Joseph's Healthcare Hamilton's West 5th Campus, which opened in February 2014. Though Century Manor is a perfect example of Victorian Gothic architecture, it has sat vacant for more than twenty years, and the subject of its preservation and future use is a controversial one. It's also provided plenty of fodder for spooky stories, and tales of eerily echoing cries from patients long passed are whispered among those who have found themselves in the shadow of this historic building.

The last remaining building from the Hamilton Asylum for the Insane, Century Manor, has sat vacant for more than twenty years.

The Hamilton Asylum for the Insane (also known as the Ontario Hospital and, later, Hamilton Psychiatric Hospital) opened in 1876 on 529 acres of land adjacent to the escarpment on Hamilton's west mountain. Perched in a lush landscape of grass and trees high above the city's brow, this magnificent setting was relatively isolated and was, until well into the twentieth century, only accessible by a dirt road.

Although it was initially intended for "inebriates" (alcoholics), the hospital began to fill with mentally disturbed patients, and the housing and treatment of that particular sort of patient became its primary function. With the next nearest asylums located in Toronto and in London, this location served patients from the city of Hamilton, as well as the ten surrounding counties.

The location was self-sufficient; an adjacent farm was complete with chickens, pigs, and cattle, as well as fruits and vegetables, and the site also had its own butcher, bakery, tailor, fire hall, skating and curling rinks, tennis courts, and chapel.

In an article by Mary Nolan about the manor (*Hamilton Spectator*, August 28, 2010), a letter to the superintendent, dated March 14, 1876 (just after the hospital opened), was quoted. It read: "On Friday ... I propose to send up twenty male and ten female lunatics ... of course, this first batch will all be good workers and perfectly quiet so you will be able to utilize their labour in putting the Asylum in order for the reception of another batch that will follow next week."

Part of a cluster of buildings that included the Barton building and the Orchard House, the "East House" (the building now known as Century Manor) was opened in 1884 to serve as a "reception hospital." This meant that people could walk in off the street without needing a physician's referral. However, just as the original buildings had been intended to serve inebriates but ended up housing the mentally ill, the East House's function evolved from its original intention: it became home to Ontario's criminally insane.

In 1890 the hospital housed 915 patients and employed as many as 119 persons. By 1902 a training school for psychiatric nursing was established there. It was accredited in 1924, and more than 240 nurses graduated from the facility before it closed in 1956.

Back in the day, treatments for mental illness were significantly more barbaric and living conditions at mental institutions were not ideal. Cruelty and injustice seemed to be par for the course for those whose plight brought them into the realm of a mental institution. Electroconvulsive therapies, described in the same *Hamilton Spectator* article as "jumper cables for the brain," were cutting edge treatments that were implemented often. The Hamilton Psychiatric Hospital Museum, now located near the Century Manor building, displays leather wrist constraints, irrigation syringes, and a trephine, a circular instrument used to saw holes in a patient's skull, all of which were once used on patients.

Electroconvulsive therapy and lobotomies were just some of the disturbing things that happened to patients. According to an article by Haunted Hamilton founder and owner Stephanie Lechniak, there was actually a time in the city's history where "lunatic watching" was a common pastime. Families would drive up the mountain from the city below with picnic baskets in order to watch, and sometimes even taunt, the patients as a way to enjoy a sunny afternoon.

The asylum was just another part of the local neighbourhood, but a large steam whistle was installed in the asylum's main building to warn local residents whenever a dangerous patient escaped. Upon hearing the whistle people would bring their children inside and lock their doors.

Considering the deplorable conditions and treatments of patients in the building during its history, is there any wonder Century Manor is long reputed to be haunted? Some even believe that tormented spirits linger to haunt both the grounds and the last remaining building.

Lechniak shared a story she'd heard from a close friend who was modelling for a photo shoot inside the old building. It started when an old steel bedpan appeared in the middle of the floor of a previously empty hallway during the photo shoot. That alone was eerie and strange, but five minutes later, while they were taking photos in a room just off that hallway, they heard the distinct echo of dragging steel coming from the hall. They looked to see if there was somebody else in the building but determined that nobody was there. However, the steel bedpan they'd spotted earlier had been moved.

In a December 2014 YouTube video entitled "Ghost Scream at an Insane Asylum," *Ghost Walks* host Daniel Cumerlato shared an audio recording that had been sent to him. In it a group of teenagers are walking around outside the vacant building, likely daring one another to get closer to the allegedly haunted locale, when one of them whispers the words, "Is there anyone here?" A distinct scream that sounds like it might be coming from a child can be heard faintly in the background.

Another chilling story was shared by an audience member at a library talk about haunted locations in Hamilton given by *Haunted Hospitals* co-author Mark Leslie in the fall of 2015. We'll call the storyteller "Martin."

Prior to when the buildings were boarded up and vacated, Martin took on a second job as a security guard to bring in some extra income. This eventually led him to working an overnight shift at the Hamilton Psychiatric Hospital.

"I was often tired from having already worked a full day," Martin said. So he looked forward to the walking patrols that would keep him on his feet and moving around. To sit for a moment would bring with it the temptation to close his eyes just for a few minutes, and that would be it. "But the walking, the constant moving, allowed me to stay alert."

Martin's job was to patrol the abandoned buildings and tunnels in search of trespassers. While performing this work he experienced two distinctly disturbing events that caused him to visibly shudder even while he was relaying the tales to Mark.

At one point during his rounds, he got a bit turned around and ended up slightly lost in a long dead-end passageway. The tunnel ended in a single old wooden door.

As he looked back down the long hallway, realizing it hadn't been his original path, he thought he heard a muffled noise. He paused and turned his head, listening.

From somewhere down the long dark corridor, most likely from behind the wooden door at the end, Martin was certain he could hear the muffled sounds of two or more people speaking. "Trespassers," he thought, and a trickle of adrenaline coursed through his veins, bringing him to full alert as he began to make his way down the empty dark hallway.

As he got closer, the voices grew louder and he figured he would find a pair of mischievous, thrill-seeking teenagers who had snuck into the buildings to do some late-night exploring.

When Martin reached the door, he took a deep breath, preparing for the speakers to flee the moment he spotted them. Then he reached for the door and opened it.

As he opened the door, Martin didn't see two startled teenagers caught in the act of sneaking around in the dark. Instead, he saw two women dressed in what appeared to be old-fashioned nurse costumes and engaged in deep conversation. Both of their heads turned to regard him as he stepped into the room.

The two women stared silently at him for a moment before one turned back to the other and said, "See, I told you he would find us."

Unable to speak or even move, Martin felt an odd chill run the length of his spine as he stared at the two of them for a moment. Then he backed slowly out of the room and closed the door again.

Standing outside the door, Martin tried to catch his breath and determine what, exactly, he had seen. He paused for a moment, working up the courage to open the door again. When he no longer heard any noise from the other side, he slowly opened the door.

Martin was further startled to find that the room was completely empty. The two nurses he had seen had vanished. And the only exit to the room was the door that he was standing in.

An even colder chill raced down his spine.

Later that same evening, still stunned and confused about whether he had imagined the two nurses in that dark room and the sound of their voices, Martin was walking through a long stretch of the underground tunnel when he felt a shift in the atmosphere.

"You know the wind pressure that you sometimes feel when you try to open a door and there's another open door or window across the room that's sucking the air out and pulling at the door?" Martin asked by way of explanation. "It felt something like that."

Martin described the hallway as both feeling and sounding like a wind tunnel. He felt an odd and overpowering pressure charging through the tunnel from behind him. He looked back and couldn't see anything out of the ordinary, but the atmospheric pressure seemed to be building. He hurried his pace down the hallway, and just as the pressure seemed to reach its peak, he felt something push hard against his back, forcing him to advance even more quickly. Within another second the noise and the air pressure ceased completely. But Martin had had enough.

After the second incident Martin left the grounds of the hospital, walked to the nearest pay phone, and called his boss to declare that he was finished at the Hamilton Psychiatric Hospital. While he would happily work at any other location as a security guard, he was not willing to set foot in those haunted buildings ever again.

Century Manor itself hasn't been used since 2009 as part of a Doors Open Hamilton event, during which approximately seven hundred people toured the building. And in 2014 Infrastructure Ontario (the provincial ministry for public infrastructure) denied a request from Hamilton heritage advocates to have a look inside the building, citing potential health and safety risks.

In a *CBC News* article, retired psychiatric worker and local heritage advocate Patricia Saunders said the building looked fine when she cleaned it up for the 2009 Doors Open Hamilton event. She expressed fears that the province was committing what is called "demolition by neglect," and actively petitioned for a task force to be revived, worried that the grand old building would be demolished like the other buildings on that property and so many other heritage landmark buildings in Hamilton.

Despite all of the stories about the building being haunted, despite the fact that it has sat empty for more than twenty years, and despite its condition as a neglected derelict with boarded up windows, weathered and rusted railings, and crumbling columns, there is still interest in the old Century Manor building. Core Urban Inc., a development company, expressed its desire to turn the building into student housing for the nearby Mohawk College when Infrastructure Ontario finally put the property up for sale in March 2015.

Steve Kulakowsky, a partner at Core Urban Inc., wants to preserve the building's heritage. As he told *CBC News*, "We're interested in it because we support the heritage of Hamilton. We also support purpose-built

Developers have been looking at renovating Century Manor into a student residence, with a redesign that has been called "innovative and inspired." In these discussions, there has been no mention, however, of the fact that the building is, perhaps, haunted.

student housing. This project would be a way of mitigating more single family homes being converted, and saving a heritage building.

"There are so many buildings in Hamilton that have been lost over time. It's a significant building. It has nice architecture. Kids don't need to live in a refurbished dorm residence. They can live in something that's innovative and inspired."

Based on the rich and dark history of the building and the nearby grounds of the former Hamilton Asylum for the Insane, one wonders what sorts of images and eerie new learnings might be inspired if a student residence does eventually open in the building.

Kreepy Kingston Hospitals

Kingston

Kingston, a small city in Eastern Ontario, takes great pride in its past and in its beautiful, well-preserved historical public buildings and houses. The city's location, at the base of the Rideau Canal and the beginning of the St. Lawrence River, ensured its place as a primary military and economic centre of Upper Canada. This is captured in the city's motto, which describes Kingston as a place "where history and innovation thrive." Along with Kingston's rich history comes a plethora of ghostly tales.

The Historical Haunting Spirits at Hotel Dieu Hospital

Glen Shackleton's book *Ghosts of Kingston: From the Files of the Haunted Walk* contains many stories about haunted locales around the city of Kingston. One of those describes the spirit of an older woman, dressed in traditional nun clothing, who is said to still be making rounds in the wee hours of the night, continuing to check on patients long after her own death. This nun is one of several ghosts reported to be seen and heard at Hotel Dieu Hospital.

The Hotel Dieu, still operational and one of the more prominent hospitals in Kingston today, was founded by the Religious Hospitallers of St. Joseph. It was built in 1845 on the corner of Brock and Sydenham Streets. In 1892 the hospital moved to its current location at 166 Brock Street, almost quadrupling the space for patients to 150. A chapel and convent were added in 1895 and 1897 respectively, and in 1912 a School of Nursing was started.

The old nun mentioned above is the most famous ghost from this location, but she has not been given a consistent name, simply referred to as the old nun. Multiple staff members have reported seeing her over the years in various locations throughout the hospital, either moving along the hallway, caught in a peripheral flicker of vision from the corner of their eye, or seen full on as a very clear image, not at all spectral-like and easily mistaken for a living person — until she inexplicably disappears around a corner or vanishes in a moment.

The spirit of a nun is one of the ghosts said to still be making the rounds in the wee hours of the night at the Hotel Dieu Hospital.

Patients have also reported being visited in the middle of the night by a woman matching the nun's description; their stories are never about feeling alarmed, but rather about being comforted by her presence as she entered their room, stood by their bedside, and behaved just like a nurse doing late-night check-ins on the patients. It is only after learning the next morning that there was no nun on duty the night before that the patients realize they've had a paranormal encounter.

There appears to be only one reported incident involving the nun when the person who encountered her was upset and frightened. A staff member reported an eerie occurrence during one of her overnight shifts. While she was pushing a cart down a quiet, deserted hallway, she was suddenly overcome by the distinct feeling that she wasn't alone. She felt immediately frightened, and as she paused in the hall, she felt a hand grasp her shoulder firmly, pulling to turn her around. There, standing before the frightened employee, was the old nun. Her image was clear one moment, but it faded the next.

The woman claimed there was nothing particularly frightening about the old nun's appearance and that, in fact, her face denoted a friendly demeanour, yet the staff member was still overcome with fright and admitted to fleeing down the hallway.

One of the most active spirits in Hotel Dieu is known by the name "Minnie." She appears in the guise of a young girl and seems to move actively about the hospital, much like a playful child.

Minnie is thought to be the ghost of a young person who was orphaned when, on route from Ireland to Canada, her parents died before arriving in the new land. Minnie, like so many other children in her situation, survived in a role that is known as a "home girl," a child forced into domestic slave labour. These children spent their days cleaning, tidying, doing laundry, and cooking in exchange for having food and a place to stay at the hospital.

Perhaps Minnie, whose playful childhood was absorbed with tedious hours of physical labour, has returned to the hospital to relive the type of childhood she longed for in the lonely years she spent without her family. Does Minnie perhaps see the current patients and staff whom she appears to as potential playmates from this lost childhood?

Today Hotel Dieu contains displays about the history of nursing and houses a room filled with acquisitions from the profession. Looking at the two different historical nursing uniforms in the display room of the building, it is easy to imagine the building's history and to speculate about the afterimages of those who used to spend time within its walls. The echoes of so many who dedicated their lives to caring for the living, or who received care at the Hotel Dieu, are occasionally seen by those living today.

The Broken Elevator and Broken Heart of Mrs. White at Kingston General Hospital

Glen Shackleton's *Ghosts of Kingston* tells a sad tale, originally reported by a Queen's University student, of a lost love, and the permanence of that love beyond the realm of this mortal coil.

The story originates in the spring of 1957 on the waterfront path across the street from Kingston General Hospital (KGH). The young student and her boyfriend were walking hand in hand along the path when they ran into an elderly woman that she recognized from her workplace. The woman (whom we will call "Mrs. White") hadn't been at work for several months as she had taken a leave in order to care for her ailing husband.

Mrs. White looked terribly distraught, and she greeted the young woman without once acknowledging or speaking to her boyfriend. She had just been to the hospital across the street to visit her husband, but the elevator in Victory Wing, where he was located, was broken, and she could not get up to see him.

The Queen's student was unsure what to say but offered her condolences to Mrs. White before they parted ways, and she continued on the walk with her boyfriend.

A week later the young student was reading a monthly magazine from Queen's when she came across an obituary for both Mrs. White and her husband. Her heart dropped when she realized the date of Mrs. White's death: three weeks earlier, which meant that she had encountered Mrs. White two weeks after the old woman had died.

Confused, frightened, and unsure what to do, the student headed to the hospital to see if the dates were wrong in the printed obituary. Her investigation revealed that Mrs. White had indeed died on the date printed, and before her death on that day, Mrs. White had been to the hospital to visit her husband. During that visit she had been informed that his illness was fatal, that he did not have much time, and that she should say her final goodbyes.

Completely distraught, Mrs. White had exited the hospital. Out on the street, her heart filled with hopelessness and grief, she walked straight into Lake Ontario, where she drowned herself.

The student also learned another intriguing fact. The elevator in the Victory Wing had indeed been broken, but it had only stopped working *after* Mrs. White's death. Was the ghost of Mrs. White continuing the routine of visiting her beloved husband, even though neither of them were still alive? Once the elevator had broken down, was the ghost unable to following Mrs. White's usual path? Since there have been no other reports of the ghost of Mrs. White visiting the hospital, could the broken elevator have forced her to finally move on?

Another ghost at KGH is seen from time to time in the emergency ward. While there are not many details to support the stories, staff claim to have seen the ghost of a man who had died shortly after his Model T Ford crashed into a tree on the exact location where the emergency room now stands. Would he have survived had he crashed his car at a later time, when he would have been so close to the life-saving help he'd needed? Perhaps that's what this ghost is looking for, forever suffering through the knowledge of being so close to proper medical attention yet unable to change his wretched fate.

St. Mary's of the Lake

Shackleton's *Ghosts of Kingston* also shares stories about hauntings associated with St. Mary's of the Lake Hospital. Established in 1946, St. Mary's of the Lake, located on Union Street in Kingston, is a teaching hospital that specializes in rehabilitation, palliative care, continuing care, and geriatric services. Almost all of the reported ghostly sightings have occurred in the oldest wing of St. Mary's of the Lake.

Staff in this hospital have repeatedly reported the ringing of patient bells coming from vacant rooms and lights that seem to turn on and off by themselves for no detectable reason. Staff have also reported bathroom taps turning on full blast all by themselves. Once this even caused flooding on one of the floors. While some believe the flooding might have been caused by a mischievous or forgetful patient, all of the patients in the wing where it occurred are in chronic care and unable to get out of their beds.

Both patients and staff have reported sightings of a woman dressed all in white. Patients claim to have seen her sitting on the ends of their beds. Though she seems almost to be waiting patiently at the bedside of a loved one, she usually disappears seconds after being seen.

She is also reported to have placed a hand firmly on the shoulders of those in need of comfort. As with sightings of her on the end of a patient's bed, when the consoled person turns to see whose hand is providing comfort, the woman is visible for the briefest of seconds before she fades away.

Perhaps the most chilling tale from St. Mary's of the Lake has to do with the eerie sound of babies crying. The noise of a helpless crying baby in the night is difficult for anyone to listen to. Humans are innately programmed, it seems, to respond to such an alarming call. However, though the wails of crying infants sometimes echo down the hallways in the middle of the night, and their desperate crying cannot be answered — there are no longer any babies at St. Mary's of the Lake.

There haven't been infants in that building since the 1940s, and earlier when the building was actually used as an orphanage. In those days, fatalities from childhood diseases were more common, so perhaps the reports from staff of being haunted by those pleading infant cries in the night are echoes from the past of children who can no longer be cared for nor helped.

Kingston Psychiatric Hospital/Rockwood Insane Asylum

Apparitions of former patients and physicians have been seen and disembodied voices, sharp bangs, and phantom screams have been heard echoing through the night at the old Rockwood Insane Asylum.

Now vacant, the former Rockwood Insane Asylum sprawls upon a lush and beautiful green space that slopes down to the shore of Lake Ontario. This set of beautiful, large structures are haunting in two ways, both as an unsettling reminder of the significant role it played in the history of patient treatment care in Ontario and Canada, and in the eerie tales that are whispered about the ghosts, spirits, and other echoes from the past that have been seen and heard within their walls.

According to the Museum of Health Care in Kingston, Rockwood Insane Asylum was originally intended to be a building that would house the criminally insane of Kingston Penitentiary. Construction of the asylum began in 1859, and the beautiful view and proximity to Lake Ontario was intended to have a calming effect on the patients housed there.

Before the Crown purchased thirty-five acres of the Rockwood Estate (originally owned by John Cartwright), a physician named John Palmer Litchfield rented the Rockwood villas as a private asylum. While Litchfield, the only physician during the early years at Rockwood, was

The now-vacant Rockwood Insane Asylum still haunts the shores of Lake Ontario, reminding those who pass it of the history of patient care in Ontario.

said to have relied heavily upon a liberal use of alcohol by day and sedative by night for patient control, he had clear viewpoints about the quality care and therapy required for the patients.

Litchfield believed that successful therapy depended upon two things: a trusting relationship established with patients, and the careful observation and classification of their ailments. He asserted that criminal lunatics were no more dangerous or violent than non-criminal lunatics and should, therefore, be treated like regular patients. This led to his position that the asylum, which originally housed only the criminally insane prisoners from nearby Kingston Penitentiary, be open to non-criminals. Litchfield contended that non-criminal lunatics were being falsely charged with criminal offences — with the support of these inmates' families, no less — so that they could be admitted to the local asylum rather than shipped off to the Provincial Lunatic Asylum in Toronto. In 1868 the Government of Ontario accepted Litchfield's proposal and the institution was opened to non-criminals.

Litchfield's successor, Dr. Dickson, was vehemently opposed to the idea of mixing non-criminals and criminals in the same building, and he insisted that they be kept apart. According to Dickson, "the criminal and non-criminal classes of lunatics should never, under any circumstances, be admitted for treatment to the same building," and they "should never be permitted to commingle" due to the fact that "one vicious criminal is sufficient to contaminate a whole ward full."

Convicts from the nearby Kingston Penitentiary were conscripted to build architect William Coverdale's progressive limestone edifice. Coverdale's design incorporated large rooms with windows and several common sitting rooms. The building was also equipped with one of the very first central heating systems in Canada. Such systems were considered far safer than stones or open fires.

The inspiring architecture and picturesque location were a source of pride for the local community, and Rockwood Insane Asylum was regularly featured on postcards from the 1900s. The lakeside location, according to Shackleton, was also a popular destination for tourists and other visitors to the Kingston area, some days in overwhelming capacity. "We have been deluged with visitors," a superintendent wrote in 1882 after about one thousand visitors came through on a public day.

While the exterior may draw tourists and captivate historians, there might be dark, unseen forces lurking inside the walls.

Over the years staff at the institution have reported being overcome by overwhelming sensations of despair and terrible dread when working in the basement, for example. Some reported feeling as if they were being smothered in a heavy blanket of negative emotions while others felt trapped and helpless.

Working alone in a particular wing of the building late at night, one employee reported a paranormal sighting. He was walking down a hallway when he rounded a corner and saw what appeared to be the figures of a mother and her young child. They stood holding hands in the main entrance doorway at the top of the stairs.

The building was locked tight, and the only other person on duty that night was a fellow employee in another wing, so the employee knew that it was impossible for anyone to have gotten inside. He became immediately overwhelmed by an eerie sensation, particularly when his eyes adjusted to the light and he detected the clothing the two were wearing. Their garments looked more like period costumes than anything a modern mother and child might be wearing.

He knew for certain that the two were not intruders in the building. In fact, he felt certain they were not real live people at all and felt himself grow weak and pale at the thought that he was looking upon a pair of ghostly visitors. Shaken, trembling, and pale, he slowly and carefully backed away down the hall, not taking his eyes off of the unmoving pair until he rounded the corner and they were out of sight.

On the Haunted North America website, under a listing for the Rockwood Asylum for the Criminally Insane, a testimonial from someone identified only as AH referenced her brother's experience doing construction and restoration work in the building.

According to AH, the construction worker reported hearing footsteps and doors opening and closing on their own. But perhaps more disturbing is the description of a photograph of the vacant building taken in the early morning hours before the sun came up. In the photograph an unexplained lime-green light can be seen glowing from the first-floor window. In the light there appears to be the shape of a person standing in the window.

Perhaps the greatest tragedy stems from one of the significant triumphs to have taken place at Rockwood. There were two medical superintendents at the institution, Dr. William Metcalf (1872–82) and Dr. Charles Clarke (1882–1905), whose perspectives as physicians were heavily influenced by the work of Dr. Joseph Workman, the superintendent of Toronto's Provincial Lunatic Asylum from 1853 to 1875. Metcalf and Clarke began a course of improving both the living conditions and treatments of the patients.

In the early 1800s the main goal of treatments at the facility was to calm the patients rather than to cure or treat them. Alcohol and chloral hydrate were the drugs of choice administered to pacify patients. Highly excited patients might also be bled as a method of calming them down.

Bound in shackles or muffs — a restraint that held two hands together in a single boxing glove–sized contraption — some patients were constantly impeded from movement. Others were treated to a continuous "bath therapy," an immersion in water with only their heads left poking up through a canvas opening for up to twelve hours at a time. These were the methods of calming more excitable patients.

Sedatives commonly used on patients included morphine, bromides, paraldehyde, sulphonal, and barbital. Physicians in the early days also performed some of the first neurosurgical procedures on Rockwood patients, using trepanning sets to drill holes into the patients' skulls.

Dr. William Metcalf was an instrumental force in reshaping the institution, transitioning Rockwood from its previous ties to the Kingston Penitentiary as an asylum for criminal lunatics to a facility more in line with other hospitals for the mentally ill. He focused on developing a program of humane treatments for the patients, abolished the overly common use of physical restraints, and instituted a program of recreational and occupational activities. Additionally, Metcalf improved the bedding, furniture, and decors of the surroundings and eliminated the use of the distinctive canvas clothing that clearly marked the patients as "lunatics." The previously used tin cups and spoons were replaced with ceramic plates and proper cutlery, and health care, religion, and education were also introduced.

Metcalf was also key in influencing his friend and future brother-in-law, Dr. Charles Clarke, to come to the institution as assistant superintendent. Together they worked at bettering the conditions for patients at the hospital, including increasing the patients' sense of freedom with the implementation of an open door policy (inspired by the work of Dr. Richard Maurice Bucke, who implemented a similar policy at the London Asylum in 1882).

In the morning hours of August 13, 1885, while both doctors were making their rounds, a patient by the name of Patrick Maloney, who suffered from an extreme state of paranoia, attacked Dr. Metcalf with a knife. Maloney stabbed Dr. Metcalf in the abdomen. Metcalf managed to survive for a few days under hospital care, but he succumbed to his injuries on August 16, 1885.

Before the building's final closure in 1995 the most commonly reported ghostly apparition occurred on the upper floors of the building. According to staff, the ghost most often seen in those areas was a stately looking man dressed in nineteenth century clothing. He was seen patrolling the hallways and moving in and out of patient rooms, as if checking on them. Many staff who have seen the gentleman believe him to be the ghost of Dr. William Metcalf.

It is both touching and haunting to think that the ghost of Dr. Metcalf, a man who changed the face and nature of the treatment inside Rockwood Insane Asylum, continued to care about the facility, even after his brutal murder. If the stately man described by so many is indeed the ghost of Dr. Metcalf, has he never given up feeling responsible for the patients he cared for in life?

As one reflects on the thousands of tortured souls who suffered and died inside the building, it is perhaps a relief to know that there is one spirit who continues to do his rounds through the dark of night, looking out for all of them for all eternity.

Ottawa Civic Hospital: An Infinite Vocation

Ottawa

Originally known as the Ottawa Civic Hospital, the Civic Campus of the Ottawa Hospital is located in the Kitchissippi Ward in central Ottawa, near the intersection of Carling and Parkdale Avenues. It first opened in 1924 with 550 beds, 88 medical staff members, 30 nurses, and 140 student nurses.

In this tale, which was shared verbally with the authors, the nurses and nursing students are of particular interest. That's because nursing is often seen as a calling or vocation, rather than simply a job or a career. These are people who dedicate their lives to the intricate dance of caring for, and relating and responding to the mental and physical needs of others. Often working extended shifts of twelve hours or longer, for a committed and engaged nurse it may seem that the ongoing call of nursing never fades. Some nurses, so utterly consigned to their vocation, might never leave, even after their physical bodies return to the earth.

One particular story from the Ottawa Civic Hospital involves a woman we will call "Aunt Shirl," who woke groggy from an operation.

As she recovered a sense of her surroundings, Shirl became aware that somebody was moving about the room.

"Oh, good," she thought. Her throat was dry — a post-operation after-effect of the anaesthesia that had put her under. "Perhaps I can get the nurse to fetch me some ice."

Shirl waved a hand at the feminine figure she saw standing across the room at the foot of her neighbour's bed, but the nurse didn't turn to acknowledge her. As Shirl's eyesight came into sharper focus, she was startled to see that the woman wasn't wearing the typical uniform of the day, but rather an old-fashioned nursing cap from long ago.

Shirl lay in the bed watching the figure of the nurse and tried to understand if perhaps there was an anniversary or special event commemorating the history of nursing — anything that might explain this particular nurse's costume. Then, apparently finished checking on the patient in the other bed, the figure turned away, as if to leave the room, and faded from sight.

Shirl was slightly taken aback, but not afraid. She mused that she had perhaps seen the spirit of a former nurse continuing to make her rounds, and checking on patients from the afterlife. Shirl wasn't frightened by the experience, instead choosing to reflect on the dedication that particular nurse must have had during her life.

St. Joseph's Hospital: Ghostly Giggles

Sudbury

Of late the site has become an $80-million-condo project headed up by Panoramic Properties and approved by the city's planning committee in October 2012. But the former location of the Sudbury General Hospital on Paris Street, now nothing but an old, empty building, quietly holds the secrets and whispers from the many births and deaths that took place in the building over the years.

Based on some of the stories told about the site, we're not convinced any amount of new construction and beautiful architecture will ever shake the spirits free from this allegedly haunted ground.

In 1944 the Sisters of St. Joseph of Sault Ste. Marie purchased seven acres of property in Sudbury at 700 Paris Street. The land was acquired to establish the Sudbury General Hospital of the Immaculate Heart of Mary. In May 1949 the cornerstone was laid, and construction was completed in 1950. Known over the years as both the Sudbury General Hospital and St. Joseph's Health Centre, the location was also home to the Marymount School of Nursing, which opened in 1953, and to the St. Joseph's Covenant in 1957. By the 1960s the hospital contained 326 beds, and a nuclear medicine department and ICU had opened. With the completion of the A-wing, the hospital could accommodate 375 patients by 1973. That same year an inquest into the mysterious death of twenty-two patients in the new A-wing was held; the deaths were believed to have been caused by a mix-up involving pipes that contained pure oxygen and nitrous oxide.

By 1997 Ontario's Health Services Restructuring Commission consolidated Sudbury's three hospitals into a single location at the Laurentian Hospital site, with a plan to close the General and Memorial Hospital locations. The old General Hospital site was maintained by the Sisters of St. Joseph, who planned to convert the building into a long-term care facility for seniors. However, after it was determined that bringing the building up to code would be too costly, St. Joseph's Villa and Continuing Care facilities were built at different locations in 2003 and 2009 respectively.

The old hospital on Paris Street operated until March of 2010. Later that spring a local photographer we'll call "Tom" and a small group of people were given permission to walk the hallways of the abandoned building, which had, since its closure, suffered from neglect and vandalism.

Though the building was locked and abandoned, Tom felt right away that the location still hummed with a strong energy, and the security guards who worked there admitted that they, too, could feel the building's strange energy.

The energy was also represented visually in the messages that former staff members had left on the walls. Though they no long traversed the hallways, the staff had left an amazing legacy of fond handwritten messages on the walls, heartfelt farewells. "It's like a going away card," Tom said, remarking about the varied scrawled messages. He also noted how the etchings on the walls added to the spooky aura of the abandoned building.

Tom's first visit took place in the early evening. He was exploring the top floor of the south-wing building when a breeze passed over his head. He paused, completely stunned, and wondered where the movement had come from — all of the windows on that floor were closed and secured. He examined the area to see if anything was open enough to have caused the odd stirring in the air, but he found no possible explanation for the breeze.

On a subsequent visit in April, Tom visited the former emergency room waiting area to take pictures of discarded hospital equipment that was stored there. He noticed an electronic sign that could not possibly have been hooked up to any computers or data-storage systems, but it was lit up to indicate that patient eighty-six was next to be served.

"All there was in emerge' was a computer and a desk," Tom said. "There's no way the sign would have been connected to anything." When he returned in June, the sign, which had indicated a readiness to see patient eight-six in April, had advanced to patient ninety-one.

Though these are odd and unexplainable occurrences, it wasn't until Tom visited the sub-basement of the hospital that he experienced something chilling he will never forget.

Tom reported that the basement was so cold that he could almost see his breath. Given that it was early summer, this was particularly odd. He wasn't more than a dozen steps from the one working elevator that had brought him down to the sub-basement when he heard something that sent a chill down his spine.

"I heard this little girl giggling," Tom said. And then he described hearing, shortly after her ghostly giggles, what sounded like a bag of marbles dropping to the floor. After the alleys dropped, the girl's laughter became louder.

Terrified, and not wanting to hear or see what might happen next, Tom beat a hasty retreat out of the sub-basement and never returned to that floor again.

He did return to the hospital to take more photographs, but he mentioned that, at times, the air would change, becoming so heavy that it felt hard to breathe. "The longer the place sits," Tom said, "the spookier it gets."

The site is to be developed into a beautiful waterfront condo, but Tom has no interest in purchasing a home in that location, believing that the old hospital grounds should be left alone. "Everybody went there," Tom said. "They were born there and they died there. Energy doesn't leave. It's sacred ground."

QUEBEC

The Grey Nuns Convent:
Grey Nuns, Ghostly Children, and a Crypt on Campus

Montreal

Students living in a residence at Concordia University who have trouble falling asleep might have a very good reason for that, and it likely has nothing to do with being away from home for the first time. Some horrific tragedies took place at that location, and there are almost three hundred bodies buried in a crypt in the basement, 232 of which are bodies of "grey nuns" who were interred there.

The Grey Nuns is the name most commonly given to a group of six distinct Roman Catholic communities of women originally founded in 1737 by Saint Marguerite d'Youville, a young widowed woman. The nuns were devoted to helping others, compassionate service, charitable events, and supporting society's most vulnerable through schools, hospitals, and long-term care facilities.

By the age of thirty, d'Youville had lost four of her six children, her father, and her husband of eight years. Turning to religion, she dedicated herself to helping others. She began a small home that took in the poor, but as the group of women grew, they took on other projects, and in 1747 they took over operation of the General Hospital of Montreal.

The term "grey nuns" was derived from the original mocking nickname given to d'Youville and her sisters. *Les grises* was a term that meant both "the grey women" and "the drunken women" — meant as a reference to the founder's husband, François d'Youville, a bootlegger who had illegally sold liquor to the aboriginal population. This term stuck and was maintained as a reminder of the group's humble beginnings even as they grew and continued their charitable work.

The first native-born Canadian to be declared a saint, Marguerite D'Youville was beatified in 1959 by Pope John XXIII, who called her the "Mother of Universal Charity." She was later canonized by Pope John Paul II in 1990.

The congregation's mother house, built in 1871, housed as many as one thousand grey nuns while also serving as a hospital and orphanage. The top floor was used as a dormitory for the youth, and the lower part of the building's west wing was occupied by sick and wounded soldiers returning from the war.

According to several articles published in the *Winnipeg Free Press* in February 1918, a nighttime fire on Valentine's Day on the top storey of the building, likely triggered by electrical wiring, resulted in the deaths of at least fifty-three children from the fifth floor orphanage. While fifty-three infant bodies were identified, there was speculation in a *Concordian* article as to whether or not some children's bodies were entirely cremated in the fire.

In 2004 Concordia University acquired the building, which had been declared a historic site by then, from the nuns and began the process of converting it into a student residence.

The chapel in the building was converted to a study hall and the nuns' rooms were turned into dorm rooms. The remains buried in the building's crypt were supposed to be transferred to Île Saint-Bernard near Châteauguay, which the nuns own, but Quebec health authorities refused to allow opening and exhumation of the tombs, citing health reasons. Some of the sisters buried there had died of infectious diseases.

Chris Mota, a spokeswoman for Concordia University, told CBC in April 2013 that the crypt in the basement will be visible to the public, but only returning nuns will be able to visit it. "For the nuns, this was their life," Mota said. "This was home. This was their family. This was where they worked, where they lived.... There's a real connection here, and they will always be welcomed back."

Some who have spent time at the residence have reported eerie and strange experiences there. On October 17, 2014, the *Montreal Gazette* published a story by Mark Abley entitled "Montreal Is a City of Ghosts." In it, one student claimed that she was unable to sleep properly while staying in the building regardless of her bedtime rituals, including camomile tea or even sleeping pills. Her dreams were plagued with ghastly images — every time she closed her eyes to sleep, horrific images of tortured children being burned alive would return. She eventually moved out of the residence — the only thing that brought the nightmarish visions to an end.

Other student residents shared different types of eerie experiences when interviewed for an October 2015 article in the *Concordian*, an independent newspaper providing local news, arts, music, sports, and opinion to the local Concordia University community.

"I'm constantly feeling as though I'm sharing my space with other people," Keeara, a student, told reporter Sarah Jesmer. "There have been multiple times that I have seen both nuns and children walking around corners and standing in the lifts."

"I haven't had any experiences," said Holly, a resident, "but I've definitely felt like I haven't been alone in a room."

Kayla, another resident told CBC that she found it creepy and that there was something eerie in the building. "I feel like it's kind of like a ghost hospital," she said.

Donovan King, of Haunted Montreal Ghost Tours, said in an April 2016 interview with CBC that "students moving into residence are literally sleeping above a cemetery, literally a few metres below. A lot of students get creeped out by this." King went on to say that students have reported hearing the tramping and crying of children coming from the top floor of the building.

According to some daycare workers at the grey nuns' residence, a couple of children in the daycare have encountered and played with the same young imaginary friend. The imaginary playmate matches the description of one of the orphans who died in the 1918 fire and has been described as wearing a tattered hat and ripped, charred clothes.

The real question, given the stories of the building's past and the eerie crypt in the building's basement, is this: would you be comfortable sleeping in this residence?

Royal Victoria Hospital

Montreal

Popularly known as "the Royal Vic" or even just "the Vic," the Royal Victoria Hospital, perched on thirty-five acres near the bottom of Mount Royal in Montreal, has been an iconic landmark since it first opened in 1893.

Many historically notable surgeons are associated with the site, including Lieutenant Colonel John McCrae, author of the classic poem "In Flanders Fields"; Martin Henry Dawson, the first person in history to inject penicillin into a patient; and John Dossetor, OC, who co-coordinated the first kidney transplant in both Canada and the Commonwealth.

But Royal Victoria Hospital is also the setting for multiple stories of phantom footsteps, eerie apparitions of former patients, and odd flickering lights, as well as nurse callers being buzzed when nobody was around to press them, and the echoes of disembodied voices in deserted corridors.

The building location, overlooking the city below, might be considered Gothic and foreboding by some. Jolene Haley, an author at the Midnight Society, wrote, "It could just be me, but I always got a creepy Arkham Asylum vibe from the place," referring to the fictional psychiatric hospital that appears in DC Comics.

In 2015 the hospital operations of the Royal Victoria Hospital moved to the Glen campus of the McGill University Health Centre, all part of a ten-year plan to incorporate the old buildings into a larger vision for the university and the local community. Regardless of what happens next to the various pavilion buildings that make up the Royal Vic, there will always exist tales of strange happenings within the walls.

There are the usual miscellaneous tales of mysterious figures seen lurking in the wards, visible one moment and then fading into nothing the next, but some intriguing tales about this building have been shared over the years. The McGill University Health Centre collected some of these eerie stories, and on October 30, 2013, they shared a selection of them on their website.

One such story is about a nurse who saw something in the staff room she couldn't explain. After a long and tiring overnight shift, the nurse decided to take a quick nap during her break on a couch. While she reclined, she opened her eyes and spotted an odd wispy white substance, a smoky light above her. When she looked more closely, the white smoke appeared to be in the shape of a person standing over her. A chill ran down her spine.

"Go away," she said, slowly sitting up and bringing her legs down onto the floor. But the smoke didn't move at all.

She carefully reached forward in an attempt to dispel the smoke. Her hands passed through it, and the foggy wisps seemed to disperse. The nurse was about to lie down again, thinking she had simply woken from an odd dream, when the white wispy fog appeared again, this time with another two human-shaped apparitions.

The nurse couldn't even scream at that point but, instead, got up and left. She never saw any similar ghostly wisps of smoke like that again, but she claimed she was never tempted to lie on that couch again.

An online testimonial from a person identified only as DB appeared on the Haunted North America website. One morning when DB was a patient at the hospital in 1996, she took a walk, frustrated by her long stay and realizing, based on her scheduled release date, that she would be in the hospital for a long time recovering from surgery. Hunched over

A typical old hospital hallway.

and slowly making her way down one of the hallways, she was thinking about how badly she wanted to be finished with a hospital visit that it seemed would never end.

As DB contemplated this, she looked to her right and noticed another patient she hadn't seen before in the hospital. The older woman stood in the doorway of one of the patient rooms, her hand clutching a tall intravenous pole. She looked directly at DB.

"You really want to get out of here, don't you?" the old woman asked.

Inexplicably chilled by the woman's presence, DB found herself unable to utter a single word. She had never seen this woman before but, oddly, the woman seemed to know exactly what she had just been thinking. DB noticed the nurses' station just a few feet ahead and was struck by a feeling that she didn't want the nurses to see her speaking to this woman. She turned her head back toward the old lady and quietly nodded.

"Straighten your back," the old woman said, "and walk as fast as you can in front of the nurses' station. It's going to hurt, but then you'll be out in no time."

DB thought about this request, considered the dozen or so steps it would take to complete the task, took a deep breath, then pulled her back as straight as she could manage, and, with pain shooting through her with every step, walked as quickly as she could.

A few hours later, in the early afternoon, DB's doctor came to see her with some good news: she was healing nicely and could go home.

She never saw the strange old lady again. However, a few months later when DB returned to the hospital for a follow-up appointment, the elevator she was on stopped inexplicably on the floor where she'd had her encounter. The first thing she spotted when she stepped off the elevator was the intravenous pole, in the same spot where the old woman had clutched it. DB shook her head, wondering if there were supernatural forces at play.

The conversation in the hallway wasn't the only reason DB felt there was something special about that old lady. Earlier in her stay, shortly after her surgery, she had woken up in the middle of the night in a pool of blood all over the bedsheets and her pajamas. Believing her stitches had come open while she'd slept, she rang for the nurse, who arrived and, seeing the blood, called for assistance. But when the nurses checked on her bandages, they found both the bandages and her stiches completely intact. The blood coating the sheets and pajamas wasn't DB's at all. Nobody could figure out where the blood had come from, but later, after some blood work, it was determined that she was anemic and needed two pints of blood transfused.

DB believes that some presence in that hospital, apparently appearing in the guises of the old woman and the mysteriously appearing blood, was constantly looking out for her.

Another one of the spooky stories posted on the McGill University Health Centre's website came from a former staff member. She shared a story about a patient who had passed away in the M5 cardiac ward. Upon declaring his time of death, the staff arranged the body, left the room, and closed the door behind them to wait for his family. When the family arrived and wanted to get into the room, the door was inexplicably locked from the inside. Security was called and when they unlocked the door, they confirmed there was nobody in the room other than the recently deceased patient. The staff speculated that perhaps the man who had died hadn't wanted his family to see him in that condition.

Former employees at the Royal Victoria Hospital shared the eerie tale of a painting that hung on the wall in the Ross Pavilion. The painting depicted a house within a beautiful landscape, and it seemed normal enough — except for the occasions when an old woman appeared looking out of one of the windows of the house. At other times the woman was visible in the doorway of the house. The recurring appearances of the mysterious old woman in the painting was so disturbing that it was eventually removed from the wall. What happened to the painting after it was taken down is unclear.

Among the many stories that have been shared about the Royal Victoria Hospital is one that partly inspired writer Alyson Grant, a former *Montreal Gazette* journalist and Dawson College graduate, to write an absurdist play in honour of the building and its ghosts. *Progress!* premiered in fall 2015 and features two ghosts who, in the tradition of *A Christmas Carol* or *It's a Wonderful Life,* do their parts to persuade a suicidal patient, the hospital's last patient, that her life is worth living after all.

Grant thought about the hospital's closure and move to a different location, and asked herself, "What will happen to the ghosts in those buildings when they stop being what they are?"

"The original idea of the ghosts being like caretakers was based on something my sister, who was an ICU nurse at the Children's Hospital here, told me," Grant said in a *Montreal Gazette* article. A teenaged boy dying in the hospital had continually referred to a mysterious red-haired girl who kept appearing to him, helping him, comforting him. Despite the fact that the boy spoke regularly about her, nobody else had ever seen the red-haired girl. Only some time after he died did one of the staff members remember a young girl with red hair who had been a patient there and had also died. The young girl's parents continued to visit the hospital on an annual basis, almost like a pilgrimage in her honour. "I couldn't help thinking," Grant said, "what's going to happen to the red-haired girl when this hospital is closed? Where is she going to go? What's going to happen to all those other people who died here?"

Considering all of the people whose lives have been touched in the building since its inception in 1893, those questions are not only haunting but daunting to consider.

As Grant says in a CBC article, when speaking about her play that celebrates the building and its ghosts, "It's my attempt at paying homage to these buildings and to our sense of what they've been in our lives. Many Montrealers have walked these halls and had profound experiences here, either of healing or giving birth, or of death."

In 2015, Grant spoke to the *Senior Times,* saying, "Those spaces become sacred in a way, a place of grief, memory, homage, thoughtfulness, and, perhaps, after years, the release of grief."

SASKATCHEWAN

Weyburn Mental Hospital:
Notorious Treatments and Ghostly Sightings

Weyburn

The Weyburn Mental Hospital began its life as a mental hospital in 1921. Like so many other facilities at that time, though, it soon began to admit people who were, for whatever reason, simply inconvenient to their families.

This practice led to overcrowding and less-than-ideal conditions for the staff and patients. Beyond that, however, the hospital became known for extreme research experiments performed on its patients. These included psychiatric drug testing that involved the use of LSD. The hospital also favoured hydrotherapy, also known as the "water cure," where patients would be immersed, naked, in a tub of icy water before being quickly moved to a nearby tub of scalding water. Other notorious treatments included insulin therapy, electroshock therapy, and lobotomies.

Since the hospital's closure in 1971, visitors have reported hearing shuffling feet and seeing shadow people walking through the halls and darting into rooms. Some even claim to have seen a woman, where no woman should have been, either looking out windows or pacing back and forth in front of windows.

The atmosphere of the hospital reportedly makes visitors feel uneasy, and one photographer related feeling suddenly and violently sick to his stomach in some of the hallways — so much so that he could not continue down them.

THE UNITED STATES

CALIFORNIA

Wolfe Manor: Scream if You Can

Clovis

When entrepreneur and skeptic Todd Wolfe decided to build a haunted house attraction in an old abandoned hospital, he had no idea how much his life was going to change. His attraction, "Scream if You Can," offered manufactured haunts in a place where, according to some, real hauntings were already taking place. "Things started happening," Wolfe told *Fresno* magazine, "but I didn't want to tell anybody. One time, I felt a breath of air on my neck and another I was touched on my lower back." Eventually, when one of the staff members from his haunted house was pulled backward into an empty room, Wolfe says he was forced to acknowledge, to himself and other people, that his property was haunted.

There's a difficulty inherent in researching a reportedly haunted hospital when that hospital has been turned into a tourist attraction and a source of income based on those hauntings: the probability of exaggerated encounters might increase. At least some of the witnesses reporting paranormal activity at Wolfe Manor have repeated their stories in multiple online locations using exactly or nearly the same words each time. This kind of reporting does tend to imply that they are well-rehearsed or scripted, so we've made an effort to exclude those reports from this book.

The History

Wolfe Manor began its existence as a build-it-yourself mail-order house kit. No, really. Between 1908 and 1940 Sears, Roebuck and Company offered homes for sale through a mail-order catalogue. Once purchased, the houses were delivered — in pieces, of course — by train to the station nearest the house's final destination before being trucked the rest of the way. The kit that eventually became Wolfe Manor looks to be the company's fanciest model, the Magnolia.

Private owner Anthony Andriotti put the home together. According to Terry Campbell, a historian familiar with the property, the eight-thousand-square-foot mansion was beautiful, with five bedrooms, a lavish ballroom, murals on the ceilings, and even a swimming pool in the basement. Andriotti lost the house in 1926 and it stood empty until 1935, when it became the Hazelwood Sanitarium. The building functioned as a tuberculosis sanitarium until 1942, when ownership changed again and it became the Clovis Avenue Sanitarium. In the 1950s the hospital began to treat both physical and mental ailments, and a wing was added to the original mansion to increase the number of people it could accommodate.

Rumours about the mistreatment of patients abounded, including stories about people being tied up to a bed or a toilet, or even being left lying naked in the hallway. The facility was overcrowded and understaffed, and since it lacked a morgue, up to eight bodies were stored in the basement at a time until someone could come and collect them. The hospital was shut down in 1992, but its story doesn't end there because, as Campbell reported in an interview with *Fresno* magazine, "Such a dark and tragic history lends itself to paranormal happening."

The current owner of the property, Todd Wolfe, bought it in 1996 and turned it into a haunted attraction called Scream if You Can. In 2004 noise complaints forced the attraction to close, but multiple ghost-hunting television shows and paranormal investigation teams began to visit, responding to Wolfe's stories of unexplainable activity at the location. The resulting investigations solidified Wolfe Manor's reputation as one of the most haunted hospitals in America.

In 2014 the building was declared a public nuisance that wasn't up to code, and it was torn down. Wolfe, who still owns the property, has plans to build a haunted luxury hotel there.

The Basement

Since the hospital lacked an actual morgue, the basement, perpetually cool, doubled as a holding place for the dead. Bodies would be stored there until they could be picked up by the appropriate authorities. It's little wonder, then, that the basement is where the most paranormal activity has been reported at Wolfe Manor. Many people have reported being touched by invisible forces, and not nicely. People have been pushed, punched, and scratched. According to Benjamin S. Jeffries's book *Lost in the Darkness: Life Inside the World's Most Haunted Prisons, Hospitals, and Asylums*, one worker was attacked so badly in a crawl space in the basement that he had to go to the hospital to have a neck injury treated. On a less violent note, the sound of a woman singing has been heard, even when there was nobody else on the property.

When The Atlantic Paranormal Society, or TAPS, investigated the hospital for their reality television show, *Ghost Hunters*, they had several interesting experiences in the basement.

One occurred when two investigators were hanging out in the basement talking to each other and to whatever ghosts might be nearby and able to hear them. Shortly after addressing the ghosts directly, they heard a very loud, sudden bang, followed by a softer knocking sound coming from right above them. Dashing up the stairs in search of the source, they found a fist-sized chunk of concrete at the top of the stairs. The rock hadn't been there when they went down into the basement, and the sounds they heard below could very well have corresponded with a rock of that size being thrown to the ground and bouncing before coming to rest by the stairs. If that were the case, though, who had thrown it?

Later, when the lead investigators, Grant Wilson and Jason Hawes, were down in the basement they heard a voice. It was so loud and clear that, at first, Jason thought it must have come from Grant's walkie-talkie. But Grant didn't have one on him. The voice sounded so normal, so conversational, that they immediately set to work looking for the speaker. They didn't find one.

They later replayed their recording to hear what the voice had said: "I like the one in the hat." Jason was wearing a ball cap; Grant wasn't. So apparently whoever, or whatever, decided to speak up in that basement had a favourite.

The Attic

The men from TAPS who investigated the attic had an encounter similar to the one in the basement with the rock. This time it wasn't a rock being dropped, but a stack of papers. The men were up in the attic watching the way passing cars made shadows play across the wall and discussing how they might be easily mistaken for something unnatural. Then they decided to check out one of the back rooms, and one of them said, "If you're here with us now, could you let us know?" A pile of papers fell loudly from the top of a box to the floor. After they got over their initial shock they investigated the source of the noise, found the papers, and realized what must have happened. They set the papers back on top of the box and walked, stomped, and jumped around it, trying to see if they could shake the papers loose, to no avail.

Mary's Room

There was only one bedroom on the third floor of the hospital that Tom Wolfe left furnished. Dubbed "Mary's room," they claim that the spirit of a woman named Mary inhabits the room, and if anyone disturbs or moves the furniture within it, Mary will move it back to where it was.

The Kitchen

Historian Terry Campbell reported he was guiding a tour through the kitchen when he saw a six-foot-tall figure in front of him. Originally he thought it was a tour guest, but when he looked closer he discovered that the man's face was blurry — like an out-of-focus photograph. While he watched, the figure faded from view right before his eyes. Before he even had a chance to wonder if he had been imagining things, one of the people on his tour with the same line of sight gasped and asked, "Did you see that?"

An infamous photograph was also taken in the kitchen. It shows a dark shape in the doorway, which Todd Wolfe claims is him, and a blurry dark shadow that appears to be a short humanoid just beside him. Todd claims this is the figure of a child, or a child-shaped thing. Is this a child-sized shadow person, or is it one of the man-baby ghosts said to inhabit the property?

According to *Lost in the Darkness*, several investigators have reported encounters at Wolfe Manor with spirits that resemble children in size and appearance, but have the faces of fully grown men. They tend to appear naked and have rubbery-looking beige skin, and they are occasionally accompanied by shadow people. They appear to want to interact with people, but most find their freakish appearances off-putting. These things, whatever they are, have been spotted all over the old hospital, from the first floor to the attic, and they seem to be unique to Wolfe Manor.

Linda Vista Community Hospital: The Woman in the Bloody Gown

Los Angeles

Linda Vista Community Hospital opened in 1904 as a hospital to treat railroad employees. Over time the character of its neighbourhood changed, becoming less affluent and more riddled with crime. By the 1980s the hospital was treating a disproportionately high number of gunshot wounds and stabbings, and the increase in uninsured patients forced it to close its emergency department in 1989. After the hospital shut down completely in 1991, it became a popular filming location for movies, television shows, and even music videos, and was also the subject of several paranormal investigations.

People have reported unusual or unexplainable noises and apparitions at Linda Vista. Two of the most dramatic and detailed reports came from Nick Groff of the *Ghost Adventures* television show, and a former nurse at the facility, Kimber Chase. Both claim to have had remarkably similar experiences at totally different times.

Kimber was at the hospital transferring a patient to another facility when she looked up and spotted a woman in the corner of the room. The woman was wearing a bloody hospital gown. She met Kimber's gaze and then reached toward her as though asking for help.

This is eerily similar to Nick's encounter with a similar woman at Linda Vista. After Nick saw the woman in the bloody gown who made eye contact and reached, pleadingly, toward him, he had a sketch artist draw her. When he showed that picture to Kimber, she said it was the same woman she had seen.

COLORADO

Various Locations:
Hospital and Sanatorium Ghosts of Colorado Springs

Colorado Springs

Tuberculosis is a highly infectious, deadly disease. In the 1800s tuberculosis was reported to be responsible for as many as a quarter of the deaths in Europe. Symptoms include a chronic cough, often accompanied by bloody phlegm, fever, and weight loss, the latter of which was one of the reasons it became known as "consumption." Tuberculosis is spread through the air from coughing, sneezing, speaking, and spitting.

In the early days of Colorado Springs, several hospitals and sanatoriums were built in town at a time when tuberculosis was of widespread global concern. Many physicians in the United States recommended that their patients be moved to Colorado Springs in order to regain their health, due to the town's dry climate and fresh mountain air. In the

1880s and 1890s an estimated one-third of the people living in Colorado Springs had tuberculosis.

Colorado Springs was home, at one time, to as many as seventeen different tuberculosis hospitals. Legislators in Colorado came close to passing a bill that would require those with tuberculosis (patients known as "lungers") to wear bells around their necks in order to be identified as infected. Sharing cutlery or glassware and even spitting on sidewalks became taboo at this time.

One of the former hospital locations, Montcalm Sanatorium, was built between 1895 and 1897 and burned down due to an electrical fire in 1907. It is said to be the source, according to Stephanie Waters, of several spirits which haunt Miramont Castle Museum. The museum still has one of the original tuberculosis huts on the far back corner of its upper parking lot.

In a 2007 article in the *Colorado Springs Gazette*, among the ghosts regularly spotted at this location are the black-veiled widow, whose face is spotted in mirrors, and Sister Henrietta, whose headless form is sometimes spotted roaming the hallways. Sister Henrietta was one of the Sisters of Mercy from the original tuberculosis treatment facility, and as the local lore goes, the woman hanged herself from the solarium on the third floor after learning she was pregnant.

Another ghost in the museum is a four-year-old named Jenny. This fair-skinned little girl is often seeing playing near the porcelain dolls in the gift shop.

In another report, Viola Butler, Miramont's castle keeper, said that she had heard singing coming from the tea room when the castle was completely empty.

There is also talk of the paranormal at Red Crags Manor, a tuberculosis treatment building originally built by Dr. William Bell, one of the founding fathers of Colorado Springs, and now a bed and breakfast. According to Stephanie Waters, Red Crags is haunted by another Jenny, a little girl who is often seen in a green dress standing at the end of guests' beds. Other ghosts, thought to be former patients from the location, include a soldier in a tattered uniform, who appears on the third floor, and a beautiful young woman dressed in white, who can sometimes be seen wandering across the lawn.

In 1973 a local chapter of Boy Scouts was camping in the area of the Modern Woodmen of America Sanatorium, a thousand-acre open-air campus with more than two hundred tuberculosis teepees that were designed to allow the cool mountain air to circulate around the patients. After sharing some campfire ghost stories with the scouts, including the story of Sister Henrietta from nearby Miramont Castle, the leader took a small group of brave boys on a moonlit hike. The group passed through a nearby cemetery where they witnessed what was described as millions of coloured orbs dancing among the headstones while the eerie sound of bells rang through the night. Since that night other people have reported seeing similar bizarre phantom lights and hearing the mysterious chiming bells.

During the Spanish influenza epidemic of 1918 a building on the corner of Nevada Avenue and Kiowa Street was converted into a Red Cross hospital. The adjacent building was used as a makeshift morgue to store the overflow of dead bodies, but it later became a nightclub known as the Underground. Staff of the nightclub have, over the years, reported the eerie feeling of being watched when working alone in the kitchen at night, and some have experienced things being thrown around a locked and vacant storage room. EVP recordings have captured inexplicable disembodied voices, moaning, and a man heard to say, "Help me!" There are also reports of a female ghost haunting the elevator and the upper stories of the building.

Among all the spooky locations that have at one time served as hospitals or sanatoriums in the Colorado Springs area, two are still operational and continue to house various inexplicable paranormal phenomena within their walls: the Colorado Springs Psychopathic Hospital (currently known as Cedar Springs Hospital), and St. Francis Hospital, which merged in 1989 with Penrose Hospital to create Penrose-St. Francis Health Centre.

Located at the foot of the beautiful Cheyenne Mountain, the Colorado Springs Psychopathic Hospital was built in 1924 to provide acute and residential in-patient psychiatric treatment for people of all ages.

The year the hospital opened, one of the patients was reported to shoot a pretend pistol at imaginary phantoms because the voices of aboriginal spirits allegedly buried on those lands told him to do so.

A ghost by the name of Farmer Floyd is also said to have haunted the hospital for more than sixty years. As the story goes, this thirty-eight-year-old bachelor farmer fell in love with a slightly older divorced housekeeper named Lois. Not a single day went by that Floyd didn't ask Lois to marry him. Lois tolerated his advances, but she never accepted his proposals. After some time Lois became frightened of Floyd when he went on drunken binges that would last weeks at a time. In 1947, after eight years of living in fear for her life, Lois decided to leave the area, and she secured a job at the Colorado Springs Psychopathic Hospital. Her employment not only paid well but also included a small apartment above the building's laundry room.

Lois felt safe and secure in her new life, and things had been going well for her until almost a year later, when Floyd showed up one night and asked her one last desperate time to marry him.

When Lois refused his final proposal, Floyd pulled out a pistol and shot her through the heart. He then placed the gun against his chest and fired a second bullet through his own heart. Newspaper articles across the country reported the tragic and horrific scene of the two bodies, the engagement ring, the pistol, and a love letter Floyd had written declaring that life without Lois would be unbearable.

Allegedly, the bloodstain on the floor of the apartment could not be removed no matter how many times it was painted, sanded, and primed.

Farmer Floyd's ghost has been seen stalking the grounds of the hospital at night, allegedly throwing stones at teenagers making out in the nearby parking lot. His ghostly image appears so lifelike that he is often confused for a hospital maintenance worker, at least until the bloodstains on his denim overalls become visible.

Inside the walls of St. Francis Hospital, there are many aspects to the phrase "the walls can talk."

A 2013 *Colorado Springs Gazette* article reported that thousands of notes to family members, to surgeons, and even to God were found scribbled on small scraps of paper. The papers had been slid into the cracks between the century-old bricks of the building, and the notes told both tales of tragedy and tuberculosis and stories of triumph and endless love.

In the same article, Roger Bost, a security guard from the hospital, shared stories about working the shift from 4 p.m. to midnight at the hospital and the various inexplicable things he had seen and heard over the years.

Bost said that the sounds of footsteps echoing through deserted corridors and doors opening and closing on their own have become commonplace. He had even witnessed a locked door — that was always kept locked — suddenly and inexplicably open, all of its own volition for a few moments before closing again without any human intervention.

Cast from nowhere, small child-sized shadows have been seen moving along the hospital corridor walls, and Bost shared another tale about a dark adult-sized figure stepping right out of the shadows and facing him as if staring. Both reported that the incident didn't feel dark or malevolent, but rather as though somebody was not ready to move on.

ILLINOIS

Ashmore Estates: I Will … Follow … You

Ashmore
When Nick Groff led a paranormal investigation through Ashmore Estates — an abandoned insane asylum in Ashmore, Illinois — he believes he was stalked by a shadow figure. It all began when he and his tour group were in the third-floor hallway of the old building. It was nighttime and incredibly dark, but cameraman Lee Kirkland saw a black mass creep out of one of the rooms, then dart back in. Intrigued, he suggested that Nick go into the room with the shape to investigate. Nick obliged, and the recorder he was holding in his hand captured an EVP that sounds very much like an angry voice saying, "Get out. Goddammit." Afterward, despite the fact the majority of the house was warm, people who entered that room reported feeling very cold, and they were overcome with emotions that seemed to come out of nowhere.

Recognizing the room as a potential paranormal hot spot, Nick gathered a group of the tour attendees and his camera crew together and attempted to make contact with the spirit. "Is there somebody that

People who have entered the abandoned building at Ashmore Estates are said to have felt cold and been overwhelmed with negative emotions.

followed me into this room?" he asked. Though no one heard a response in real time, Nick reported feeling a cold mass move through the room and later, upon reviewing the recording he made at the time, he heard a disembodied response to his question: "Yes ... I will ... follow ... you."

A Brief History

Like many hospitals that were founded in the early 1900s, Ashmore Estates began its existence as a poor farm meant to help society's most vulnerable. It was built in 1916 and was originally called Coles County Poor Farm. It functioned in that capacity, providing a home and sustenance for people who weren't able to provide it for themselves, until 1959 when it was bought by outside investors, renamed, and turned into a private psychiatric hospital.

During its time as Coles County Poor Farm, the operation was largely self-sufficient, and it functioned much like a hamlet or a small village. A former tenant, Nancy Andrews Swinford, described the poor farm: "They were warm and had good food on the table. And they loved working and earning their keep. They weren't moochers.... They mostly grew their own food, did their own butchering and smoked the meat. They smoked their own bacon and hams in the smoke house, they killed and dressed all their own chickens, and made their own butter."

As happens in any settlement, people died. Tenants of the Coles County Poor Farm who passed away were laid to rest in a small cemetery north of the grounds. Another slightly larger cemetery for paupers is also found nearby.

In 1902 the poor farm was inspected by the Board of State Commissioners of Public Charities, which noted that though there were insane people housed at the facility, no special arrangements were made for them. On the plus side, that meant mentally ill residents were not locked up or kept in restraints (excessive use of restraints for mentally ill people was not uncommon at the time), but depending on how disruptive or violent those tenants were, perhaps that wasn't such a positive thing for the other vulnerable people living at the farm.

At a later inspection, in 1911, the farm conditions were found to be deplorable. In particular, the inspection report condemned the vermin-infested walls and swarms of flies everywhere, especially on the inmates' food.

In 1959 Coles County Poor Farm became Ashmore Estates — a private psychiatric hospital. It operated as such until its closure in 1986.

Elva Skinner

One of the most tragic stories surrounding Ashmore Estates took place in 1880, while it was still functioning as a poor farm — the tragedy of little Elva Skinner.

When Elva's father, a Civil War veteran, passed away, her family was left impoverished, so Elva's mother packed up her three children and moved them to the only place left for them in their world — the Coles County Poor Farm. There they grieved their loss while they made themselves a new home and tried to move on with their lives. But on February 15, 1880, when Elva was only five years old, tragedy struck her family again.

Elva slept late that morning, and while nearly everyone else was downstairs eating, she woke up and stood by the fire to warm herself while she got dressed. She must have wandered too close to the flames because her clothes caught on fire and, according to newspaper reports shared on the Mysterious Heartland website, Elva was fatally injured before anyone could come to her rescue. Her life was over before it had even begun — burned to death because she chanced to stand too close to the fire on a cold winter morning.

How her mother's heart must have broken — to have already lost her husband, and then to lose her daughter in such a horrific way! But though Elva was dead, there are those who believe her spirit lives on at the abandoned hospital.

Though the building that currently inhabits the site is not the same one that stood at the time of Elva's death, EVPs at Ashmore Estates have reportedly captured the voice of a young girl pleading for help and asking for her mama. Many believe this is Elva, still trapped after all these years, wandering around the second and third floors of the hospital looking for her mother. Others say it defies logic to think the child would haunt a building she never knew in life.

Although the life and death of little Elva has been documented, reported sightings of her ghost didn't start until after 2004. Is it a coincidence that *Tales of Coles County* by Michael Kleen was published that year, over a century after Elva's death? One of the stories in Kleen's book features the ghost of Elva Skinner. Perhaps this work of fiction is the spark that fires people's imaginations about Elva, making them predisposed to hearing her voice or seeing her apparition lingering around the grounds of the abandoned hospital. If so, does that diminish the evidence of her haunting, or simply make people more open to receive it?

Whatever the truth is, we know for a fact that Elva lived and died on the land where Ashmore Estates now stands. Her story is heartbreaking, likely to haunt your memory just as she is said to haunt the hospital.

Joe Bloxum

In 1906 circumstance forced Joe Bloxum to become a resident of the poorhouse that later became Ashmore Estates. Despite how gloomy one might imagine living at a poorhouse to be, Joe, sixty-one years old at the time, reportedly made a home for himself and found contentment there. He resided at the poorhouse for fifteen years, working with the superintendent to maintain the lawns and grounds, keeping them clean and presentable.

When Joe was seventy-six, however, he took a trip to Charleston and was seen near the railroad tracks. Shortly afterward a motorist stopped to pick him up as he stumbled toward home. Joe had severe bruises around his shoulders and upper body, and the good Samaritan drove him the rest of the way home. Once there, legend says he was taken down to the boiler room to await the doctor. Since Joe would have had a bed on the premises, we must assume that they hoped the warmth in the boiler room would aid with his shock.

Though no one knows for certain, it is supposed that Joe, who was described as quite feeble, had tried to beat a train and failed. It didn't strike him head-on but side-swiped him, leaving him battered and bruised. Unfortunately, the shock and trauma from being hit overwhelmed poor Joe, and he died there in the boiler room. According to an obituary printed in the *Oakland Messenger* and reproduced on the Poorhouse Story website, Joe was buried two days later in the "little green plot" on the property.

It is said that Joe continues to haunt the place he last called home, Ashmore Estates. He appears as a shadowy apparition in the eerie corridors and his gruff voice has been captured as an EVP by paranormal investigators.

Lesley Michael, the case manager and assistant lead investigator for the Illinois Metaphysical and Paranormal Society, claims that Joe still inhabits the boiler room where he died. "Even if you're not seeing anything or actively hearing anything, you feel like you're not alone," Lesley reports. It goes beyond just feeling unseen eyes on you, however. Paranormal investigator Becky Guymon reports that the boiler room is rampant with paranormal activity. People have reported being touched or scratched, electronic equipment will act up, and things are occasionally thrown at visitors' heads. Things like light bulbs.

In fact, when television host Mark Rivera and his cameraman visited Ashmore Estates to film a Halloween special, Mark was talking with Lesley in the boiler room when his cameraman, Steve, wandered into the next room. On the footage from Steve's camera, you see the shot pan past a table cluttered with dirty wires, cables, and a light bulb. As the camera continues into the room, a clank and a curse can be heard. Steve says that somehow the light bulb flew from where it was sitting on the table and hit him in the neck. Lesley and Becky seem to think Joe is to blame, suggesting that he's usually angry and doesn't much like being "messed with."

Perhaps freakiest of all? Lesley says sometimes you can hear growls coming from the shadows.... Do they belong to Joe or to something darker? There is no way to know for sure.

Peoria State Hospital: The Legend of the Graveyard Elm

Peoria

If we work with the assumption that hospitals are so frequently haunted because of the copious amounts of emotional energy (both negative and positive) and trauma contained within their walls, Peoria State Hospital is the perfect petri dish for paranormal activity. Reading over the list of treatments that were implemented at Peoria State Hospital is like reading a timeline of psychiatric and medical treatment:

> 1902 — Colour therapy introduced
> 1903 — Light therapy introduced
> 1905 — Hydrotherapy introduced
> 1906 — Tent colonies started
> 1908 — Industrial therapy introduced
> 1909 — Phototherapy introduced
> 1930s — Syphilis outbreak treated by infecting patients
>   with malaria
> 1938 — Insulin shock therapy introduced
> 1940s — Lobotomies and trepanning performed
> 1942 — Electroconvulsive therapy (ECT) introduced
> 1951 — Occupational therapy introduced
> 1963 — Group therapy introduced

Some of those treatments, colour and light therapy, for example, are innocuous enough, but others such as lobotomies, trepanning, and ECT would be traumatic and terrifying ordeals for everyone involved, both patients and witnesses. But there's more! In addition to the deaths you would expect to be associated with a hospital, Peoria State Hospital is also connected with at least a handful of murders.

According to a page about the Peoria asylum's history from the Abandoned Whereabouts website, in 1903 a patient was allegedly beaten to death by two attendants, but the perpetrators were never charged. Several decades later, in 1967, a patient smashed a nurse in the head with a steel bar, killing her. In 1972 two patients were murdered by fellow patients: one patient was struck in the head with a chain while waiting in line for lunch and another patient was beaten to death.

Though efforts were made over the years to make the hospital as comfortable a place to live as possible, it was still the site of several outbreaks that could be attributed to poor care or supervision. For example, in 1909 a pellagra outbreak began. The outbreak lasted at least three years, affecting more than 500 patients and killing 150 of them. Caused by poor diet, pellagra is a disease that causes diarrhea, eczema (intensely itchy inflammation of the skin), and dementia. What's more, in some cases this disease also causes aggression, confusion, and emotional disturbance. Given that in 1909 the Peoria State Hospital was called the Illinois General Hospital for the Insane, one can only imagine how much the pellagra outbreak would exacerbate pre-existing conditions in the patients.

Another outbreak occurred in the 1930s, this time syphilis. Syphilis also causes skin rashes and sores, and if left untreated, it can also progress to the point where it causes dementia or death. Although penicillin, used to treat syphilis now, had been discovered in 1928, it wasn't a popular treatment for infections until 1942. Until then many different experimental treatments were used on those infected, some of which might now be considered as dangerous as the disease itself.

One such treatment, the one used at Peoria State Hospital, was to inject the patient with malaria. Malaria causes a high fever, and the hope was that the fever would combat the syphilis, effectively trading one disease for another. The note on the Peoria Asylum's website about this treatment simply said, "There were untold numbers of deaths" (viewable only via the Wayback Machine).

The hospital closed in 1973, and since then the facility's reputation has grown. Stories abound of suicides in the woods and ghostly children who play with balls, and there are many recorded EVPs. One of the most interesting stories, however, actually took place back in 1910 when the hospital was still in operation.

Old Book and the Graveyard Elm

The story begins when a man working in a printing house suffered some form of mental break that left him incapable of intelligible speech — to the point that he couldn't even tell anyone his name. Sometime before 1910 he was taken into custody by a police officer who noted in his report that the man was "a bookbinder." When the poor afflicted gentleman was checked into the Peoria State Hospital (known at that time as the Illinois Asylum for the Incurable Insane) he was signed in as A. Bookbinder. In some stories his name is said to have been Manual Bookbinder, or M. Bookbinder. Regardless, all reports agree that he quickly came to be known as "Old Book."

Though unable to speak, Old Book was otherwise strong and healthy. So when the man in charge of the hospital, George A. Zeller, conscripted patients for a burial corps, Old Book was among them. The burial corps was a group of six patients and one staff member who, as their name suggests, were responsible for digging the graves of those who died at the hospital whose remains were unclaimed by friends or family.

This hospital had been built according to what is known as a "cottage plan," which meant it was quite spread out and comprised several buildings. Thus, most of the patients didn't know one another. In fact, there was a fair chance that even the staff wouldn't know every patient, so funerals were usually relatively unemotional. The burial corps would dig the grave and then stand quietly off to the side while the funeral service was conducted. Once the funeral was done, the corps would return to the graveside to fill in the hole.

It surprised everyone when, at his very first internment, Old Book took off his cap, wiped his eyes, and then leaned against the huge old elm tree in the centre of the graveyard, letting it support his weight while he sobbed. He did this at every funeral. He would dig the grave and then, once the service began, he would doff his cap, wipe his eyes, and sob against the tree everyone called the "graveyard elm."

When the time came for Old Book's own funeral, held in the hospital cemetery, the service was remarkably well attended because Book had become a sort of local legend around the facility. Dr. Zeller himself officiated and, according to his memoir, several hundred people, including staff and patients, attended. Book's casket was suspended over the grave by two crossbeams, where it would remain until members of the burial corps lowered it into the ground at the end of the service. In Dr. Zeller's book, *Befriending the Bereft*, he wrote,

> Just as the choir finished the last lines of "Rock of Ages," the men grasped the ropes, stooped forward, and with a powerful, muscular effort, prepared to lift the coffin, in order to permit the removal of the crossbeams and allow it to gently descend into the grave. At a given signal, they heaved away the ropes and the next instant, all four lay on their backs. For the coffin, instead of offering resistance, bounded into the air like an eggshell, as if it were empty!

The scene that followed is said to have been a bit chaotic, as one would well imagine. But the spookiest part was that a loud wailing voice suddenly pierced all the commotion and confusion, drawing every eye to the place from which it emanated — the graveyard elm. There, visible to everyone attending his funeral, was Old Book. He was crying and wailing, in the words of Dr. Zeller, "with an earnestness that outrivaled anything he had ever shown before."

After a moment of stunned silence, the lid of Book's coffin was lifted off, because, surely, if Old Book were leaning against the graveyard elm, he couldn't also be dead inside the casket. The instant the lid came off the coffin, the wailing from the tree stopped. There, inside the coffin, was Old Book. Dead. And when his mourners looked once again to the tree he'd been sobbing against, they found that his apparition had vanished.

"It was awful, but it was real," Dr. Zeller wrote in *Befriending the Bereft*. "I saw it; 100 nurses saw it and 300 spectators saw it."

In his book *Lost in the Darkness*, Benjamin S. Jeffries reports that soon after Old Book's funeral the graveyard elm began to wither and die. It resisted all efforts made to save it, and a year later it was as dead as poor Old Book. However, when workmen came to remove the dead tree from the graveyard, they struck it with an axe, and an unearthly scream came from it. For years and years every attempt to remove the tree was foiled by the sound of the horrible wailing that emanated from it each time it was touched with fire or steel. Eventually nature, unpitying nature, saw to its removal when the graveyard elm was struck during a lightning storm. If not for that, the tree might still be standing today, a not-so-silent monument to one of Peoria State Hospital's most infamous and beloved patients.

INDIANA

Central State Hospital: Fear and Distortion

Indianapolis

When psychic Benjamin S. Jeffries first arrived at Central State Hospital in Indianapolis, his initial impression was of "a thick, heavy blanket made up of extreme sadness and pain." Given the history of the place, we're not especially surprised.

Formerly known as the Central Indiana Hospital for the Insane, this psychiatric hospital was opened in 1848. Back then it was one building that housed five patients, but it was situated on over one hundred acres of land, and the need for its services was so great that it continued to expand. In 1926 the name changed to Central State Hospital and by 1928 it housed around three thousand patients in several buildings. Beneath the ground, connecting the buildings, was a veritable rabbit warren of tunnels.

Allegations of Abuse

Allegations of rampant patient abuse surrounded the hospital from its earliest days right up until its closure in 1994.

One of the most persistent rumours alleges that the tunnels deep in the bowels of the facilities are more than just a way to get from one building to another. It is said that those tunnels contain dark dungeon-like rooms with chains and shackles in them, and that the more problematic patients — those who screamed uncontrollably or had violent tendencies — were frequently kept down there. Alone. In the dark. For unknown lengths of time.

Unfortunately, there is plenty of evidence to back these rumours up. Not only do hospital workmen and former employees tell stories about stumbling into these rooms today, back in 1870 the superintendent of the hospital wrote about them. In a letter to the Governor of Indiana he wrote, "Basement dungeons are dark, humid and foul, unfit for life of any kind, filled with maniacs who raved and howled like tortured beasts, for want of light and food and ordinary human associations and habiliments." No wonder. We think anyone left in those conditions would rave and howl, and the suffering of a person chained that way would be multiplied if they were already suffering from afflictions of the mind.

Interestingly, this treatment of patients was justified under the guise of a "retraining exercise." The isolation and darkness were meant to be therapeutic and to reverse the patient's insanity. Even understanding that we know a lot more about treating mental illness now than we did then, it is difficult — if not impossible — to comprehend how such treatment could be justified or considered beneficial. Thankfully, once news of these "treatments" was made public in 1894, the public outcry was such that use of restraints at the hospital was greatly limited.

Still, even those patients who weren't chained up in underground dungeons were kept in conditions that might, if one was feeling generous, be called substandard. Patients slept on straw mattresses in buildings with rotten floors and leaking roofs (one can imagine the quality of the straw under those damp conditions). Dr. Everts, the aforementioned superintendent, reported that the wards these patients were housed in were "without adequate provision for light, heat and ventilation." Patients who were lucky enough to have a bed could find themselves confined to it for days at a time. In fact, the very building was used against patients — window wells were used as tiny cages that would allow patients to be out in the sunlight but unable to walk about or escape. Frustrated in his attempts to improve the conditions at the hospital, Dr. Everts resigned in protest in 1872.

Sadly, his protest appears to have accomplished nothing. Allegations of abuse persisted until the hospital's closure. Staff members were accused of everything from rape and sexual battery to neglect and physical abuse. Though there were plenty of allegations, we were unable to find any convictions against staff members at Central State Hospital. Still, the accusations were taken seriously enough that Governor Evan Bayh ordered a full investigation into how things were done at the hospital.

In the Tunnels

Five miles of tunnels run, like a labyrinth, beneath and between the various buildings. They are dark and claustrophobic and have a history of unimaginable terror and torment. It is no wonder they are the setting for a variety of urban legends and unsettling stories.

According to Crime TV's documentary about Central State Hospital, one ghostly presence said to haunt the tunnels is the "Red Lady." The Red Lady is a nurse who used to work at the Central State Hospital. She frequently wore a red cape and did a lot of grounds checks during her shifts, to ensure no one was wandering about where they didn't belong. The story goes that while working in the old main building, the nurse was involved in a tragic, though unspecified, accident and died. Perhaps she doesn't realize that death released her from her responsibilities at the hospital because people have reported seeing the flash of her red cape when they are down in the tunnels. Further, it is said that if you're wandering around down there where she doesn't think you belong, she will touch you to let you know you're in the wrong place and to stop you from continuing on. Perhaps someone ought to find the Red Lady and tell her that her shift is over. It's okay for her to rest now.

"When Darkness Comes to Central State," a section in the book *Haunted Indiana 3* by Mark Marimen, tells several stories about eerie and unnerving events at the facility. One whispered story it recounts about the tunnels is about a nurse who, while exploring the tunnels, discovered a room with a dirt floor and manacles attached to the walls. She was disturbed by the sight and its implications, so she left immediately. However, later that year she happened to be walking by that room again when she heard the unmistakable sound of moaning coming from inside. Despite her terror at the sound, the nurse opened the door to look inside but found the room dark and barren. Shaken by the encounter, she fled the tunnels, and it was many months before she even relayed the events to her supervisor. "Oh, never mind that," the woman is reported to have said. "We all know about that room and we all stay away from it. A lot of us have heard those things."

They all knew about the room and just stayed away from it. How many people have to witness moans coming from an empty room before it becomes so commonplace that you don't even think it's unusual enough to warrant a mention?

Alvin

The story of Alvin is probably the most widely reported story from Central State Hospital, and it also has a deep connection to the tunnels. Marimen has a lot to say about Alvin.

Alvin was a low-risk patient at the hospital and, as such, was allowed to wander freely about the grounds. One day, however, he vanished. Poof. Though a thorough search was conducted, no one could find any sign of him anywhere. Because Alvin didn't pose a risk to himself or others, eventually the staff stopped looking, assuming that he'd wandered off the grounds and would simply return whenever he returned.

Sometime later, reports differ as to whether it was months or years, a woman named Agnes was admitted to the hospital. After she'd been there for a while, Agnes developed a habit of wandering off. A former nurse relayed the story:

She would just disappear from the ward and they would have to search for her. Inevitably, she would be found on the steps that lead down into the catacombs, just sitting by herself. It got to be so regular that when she disappeared, instead of calling security, they would just send one of the nurses down there to bring her back up.

Finally one of the nurses, probably tired of being sent repeatedly to collect Agnes from the stairs, asked her why she kept going down there. Agnes shrugged and said she liked to go visit her friend Alvin who lived in the tunnels.

Had Agnes given any other name for her friend the nurse might have dismissed her response as fanciful thinking or the result of a troubled mind, but Alvin was not a common name, and it reminded the nurse of the missing patient from a couple years before. Maybe Alvin hadn't left the grounds after all. Perhaps he was still there, living in the maze-like tunnels beneath their feet. If that were the case, he needed to be located and retrieved — for his own safety, as well as everyone else's. It just wouldn't do to have a mental patient, however harmless, wandering around in the tunnels beneath the hospital.

The nurse reported what Agnes had said to her superiors and another search was conducted. It was as fruitless as the first until, after several hours, one of the searchers found a partially open crawl space off the tunnels. He looked inside, and there was Alvin's body. Alvin had been dead for quite some time.

The discovery of Alvin's body brings up a lot of questions — how did it get into the claustrophobic crawl space? How did he die? But even more disquieting is that after the discovery of Alvin's corpse, Agnes stopped sneaking off to hang out on the catacomb stairs, and she never spoke about Alvin again. It was as though Alvin's spirit had been lingering, waiting for his remains to be discovered and put to rest before he could find peace.

Things that Go Bump in the Night (and Day)

One former psychiatric nurse who worked at Central State Hospital for several years claims to be an agnostic when it comes to the supernatural. She told Mark Meriman that the administration discouraged staff from sharing ghost stories — but, of course, they still did on occasion. In fact, it seems like everyone who worked there had at least one story to share. This nurse, whom Mark gave the pseudonym "Ms. Torreson," had an interesting one of her own.

Shortly before the hospital shut its doors for good, Ms. Torreson was working the late shift. Because they had been moving patients to other hospitals in preparation of Central State closing, there was a lot of commotion on the ward. Some psychiatric patients don't deal well with change, so more effort than usual was required to get them settled in bed. Around three o'clock in the morning, though, things quieted down enough that she could take a break and relax. Unfortunately, that break was cut short when Ms. Torreson heard the sound of a woman sobbing. When the nurse got up to investigate, she realized the sound was coming from a room at the end of the hallway that should have been empty — it had belonged to a patient who had already been transferred out.

She was aggravated at the thought that someone had wandered out of her room and into this empty one, but when Ms. Torreson paused outside the room, listening to the sound of sobs emanating from within, her mood changed. "There was something about it that made all the hair on my arms stand up," she said. "It was heartbreaking — like someone inside was in incredible pain or distress. But when I opened the door, the crying suddenly just stopped and there was no one there. The room was empty — even the beds were gone. I stood there and, in that moment, I was scared to death."

Ms. Torreson scurried away from the room and back to her desk, where she poured a cup of coffee and tried to convince herself that there was a logical explanation — maybe it was just the wind, or perhaps her imagination. Then she happened to look down the hallway toward where she'd heard the weeping, and she saw "this hazy kind of shadow floating in front of the room. I turned my head and stared in that direction and at that moment it zipped down the hall and disappeared into the wall at the end of the hallway."

She's not the only person to have seen something like that, either. A few years later when the hospital was empty, it was regularly patrolled by police officers. One officer was alone on the second floor when suddenly he heard a woman's high-pitched cry. Spinning around to locate its source, he saw a hazy feminine form dart through his flashlight beam. In no time at all she ran to the end of the hallway and disappeared into the wall.

Could this have been the same darting shadow that Dan T. Hall caught on video when he was investigating Central State Hospital? In Dan's footage, captured by a stationary infrared camera, a hazy shape darts in front of the camera. The shape is not quite human, but not quite inhuman. It moves fluidly, like water, though it looks more like smoke. At the other end of the hall is a door with a light reflecting from its glass window. Nothing unusual is reflected in that glass. The line of sight between it and the camera is never broken in the video, and you can always see the light reflecting. But the camera's autofocus feature was triggered and that only happens if something crosses its line of sight, so something moved in front of the camera. Did Dan capture one of the spirits that wander the halls of this behemoth of a hospital?

While researching this book, we watched hours and hours of footage from paranormal investigations, and those three seconds are Rhonda's favourite.

The Administrative Building

Strange occurrences aren't limited to just one building on the Central State campus. Former employees and patients have reported hearing unexplainable sounds, disembodied footsteps, slamming doors, and sobbing in several locations in and around the hospital, including the administrative building and the power station. One former patient, whom Dan T. Hall refers to as "Patient X" in his documentary, recalled one of the nurses who used to work at the hospital. According to Patient X, she had a very distinctive, witchlike laugh. When Dan and his crew were in those hallways filming, they captured an EVP that sounds very much like a woman's laugh. You could even call it a cackle — like a witch. There's no indication that the nurse the patient spoke of has passed away, but one could consider this laugh to be evidence that energy from its time of operation still lingers in the hospital. For good or for ill.

The groundskeeper had a haunting story that took place in the administrative building. "Before I started working here, I never believed in ghosts," he said. But now, with a few graveyard shifts under his belt, his feelings in that regard seem to have shifted. He says he's heard doors slam when no one was around and also unexplainable footsteps.

One dramatic instance of footsteps happened one night when the groundskeeper was relaxing by himself in a side room in the administrative building. This particular room had a huge glass window that overlooked the larger room it was in — possibly used by the staff to keep an eye on their patients. Out of nowhere he heard the distinctive sound of high heels click-clacking across the floor, headed straight toward him. Jumping out of his chair, he peered through the window. No one was there, but the footsteps continued to approach, right up to the other side of the glass he was looking through. The sound paused there for a moment, and then he heard the footsteps turn and walk back the way they'd come. The whole while he watched where the sounds were coming from but saw no one.

The Carpentry Building

When psychic author Benjamin S. Jeffries visited Central State Hospital in 1994, he found himself powerfully drawn to the Bahr building, which is reportedly where the criminally insane were housed. But even stronger was his attraction to the carpentry building. Situated right beside the power station, which is alleged to be a hub of spiritual activity, the carpentry building captured his attention right away.

While he was walking around it, taking photographs, Jeffries heard two men speaking. One of them said, crystal clear, "What are you doing here?" Thinking that it might be one of the hospital's guards or a policeman (Central State is situated in the middle of the city), he turned around to answer, but no one was there. Jeffries was alone, but the voice had come from so near to him that, had it come from a mundane or human source, he would have seen the speaker.

Though Jeffries investigates haunted locations all over the world and is used to brushes with the other side, he says he still gets chills when he thinks about that voice.

The Power Station

The power station is one of the areas of greatest paranormal activity at Central State Hospital. Some people believe that power stations can act as a sort of battery for ghosts, amplifying and powering them. There's more on that in the New York section about Rolling Hills Asylum ahead. The people who subscribe to this theory also tend to believe that most ghosts and hauntings are the result of residual energy left behind when people's bodies die. This would explain why entities affect electrical equipment, electromotive force (EMF) readers, and the like. It would also explain why phenomena reported near facilities that generate electricity tend to be stronger and more powerful than those reported elsewhere. Such is the case with the power station building at Central State Hospital.

The power station is one of the areas of greatest paranormal activity at Central State Hospital.

Paranormal activity in the power station tends to take the form of rattling pipes, unexplained voices, shadows, screams, and spontaneous equipment activity. In addition to those things, however, on at least one occasion a workman at the power station was physically attacked. Midway through his shift he became tired, so he found himself a comfortable place to take a nap, deep in the bowels of the power station's basement. He chose a room with only one door so that no one could sneak up on him and find him slacking off. Or so he thought.

He was jolted from sleep by the sensation of being choked. Breaking free from the stranglehold, he jumped to his feet and turned on the light to see the cowardly wretch who had attacked him in his sleep, but he found himself alone. There was no way anyone could have left the room without his noticing because he stood between the doorway and the rest of the room, but there was no one there. The workman retreated up to the light of day and told his colleague about the attack, pulling his shirt down to reveal dark red marks around his neck.

The man refused to ever go back down into that part of the power station again, even at the risk of losing his job.

While Dan T. Hall and his crew were filming in the power station they also captured several EVPs. The first was recorded shortly after one of the psychics on the team mentioned feeling a force in the basement that wanted them to leave. On the video none of the investigators or the film crew react to the voice at the time, so it's safe to assume they didn't hear it until they reviewed the footage later, but shortly after the psychic says the entity wants them to leave, the words "Go, for God's sake" can be heard in a whisper.

Once the team had exited the power station, the recording equipment they left behind captured the sound of pipes clanging. There is no logical reason for the pipes to make noise since the power station has been closed for several years. This sound is followed by an EVP of someone or something whispering, "Bye...." This makes a certain kind of sense — the kind that makes you never want to set foot in that building.

The Grove and the Grounds

Now and then patients die at a hospital, as you would expect. After all, a hospital is a place for sick people. However, they might not be expected to die outside the buildings. When Mark Marimen was writing "When Darkness Comes to Central State," he interviewed Mr. Jarecki, a former employee. Mr. Jarecki reported that at least one patient met his end in one of the beautiful ornate fountains out on the lawn. Not quite creepy enough to raise the hair on your arms? Another patient suffered a horrible death in the area of the grounds known as "the grove."

There, beneath the sprawling boughs of the trees, one patient brutally murdered another, beating him to death with a stone. The perpetrator was promptly shipped off to another facility, but there are some who believe the victim is still there — or at least some part of him remains. "When you walk by that grove of trees at night, you can still hear the screaming and moaning coming from it," said Mr. Jarecki.

Employees from the hospital also report seeing blurs of movement that they believe to be the spirits of patients running for the gate. When the hospital was operational, occasionally patients would make a run for it — trying to zip out the gates of the hospital before the guards could catch them. Are their spirits still there, trapped on the grounds and perpetually trying to escape?

Visitors to the hospital frequently report an oppressive air and a feeling that they are being watched. Perhaps Dan T. Hall said it best: "This place, its energy, began to work on all of us, stripping away the curiosity that brought us here and replacing it with fear and distortion."

KENTUCKY

Waverly Hills Sanatorium: The Most Haunted Location on Earth?

Louisville

Shadow people, spectral nurses, ghostly children, and distorted human forms crawling along ceilings: these are just some of the

Is Waverly Hills Sanatorium the most haunted building on earth?

disturbing things people have encountered at Waverly Hills Sanatorium in Louisville, Kentucky.

Originally a two-storey building, the sanatorium eventually grew to be a massive structure. In fact, in its heyday Waverly Hills was like a small city — self-sustaining and possessing its own zip code.

Waverly Hills operated as a sanatorium, or tuberculosis hospital, housing and treating over four hundred patients at a time for many years. It closed its doors in 1961 after the development of streptomycin, an anti-biotic proven to be effective in treating tuberculosis, rendered the facility obsolete. It reopened the next year as Woodhaven Geriatrics Hospital but was closed by the state in 1981 due to allegations of patient neglect and abuse. With a history like that, is it any wonder that Waverly Hills has been called one of the most haunted places on earth?

Shadow People

One thing Waverly Hills is known for is the sheer number of shadow people purported to reside within its walls. Shadow people are exactly

"Conceptual" photograph of a shadow person: an entity believed to often be formed of a darkness so dense that light cannot penetrate.

what the term implies — people-shaped shadows. Except that these shadows don't have a source — there is no one standing in a light to cast them. They just *are*. Shadow people take on several different shapes, everything from clear representations of humans to wispy or smoky mists. Though there are exceptions, usually shadow people are formed of darkness so dense that light cannot penetrate them.

Theories about what causes shadow people are widely diverse, running the gamut from overactive imaginations to ghosts, demons, aliens, or even time travellers. Whatever they are, and whatever they want, many who have witnessed a shadow person have been irrevocably changed by the experience.

The Body Chute

Waverly Hills Sanatorium is massive, and it sits atop a very big hill, so getting supplies up to it could be a nightmare. It was also a cold trip to the bottom of the hill for staff in the wintertime. To solve this problem, they built a five-hundred-foot-long tunnel from the hospital to the base of the hill. One side of the tunnel had stairs so people could get up and down; the other side was a sloped "slide" used for carts and railcars — things with wheels. In time the facility began using the tunnel to transport disturbing cargo — human bodies.

Urban legend says the tunnel found this purpose when the hospital death rate peaked — the stories say one person was dying at the facility every hour, but thankfully the real rate was much lower than that — an average of 104 deaths per year, peaking at 152 deaths per year around the end of the Second World War.

Many people attribute the unnerving feeling they get within the tunnel to the passage of so many freshly deceased; others say it is merely claustrophobia and echoes. Whatever the primary cause, people have reported disturbing shadows, the sound of footsteps, and voices that can't be explained within the tunnel's walls.

Perhaps one of the most spectacular occurrences in the body chute, or death tunnel, as some prefer to call it, happened to Brian and Justin of the Johnsdale Paranormal Group. They spent a significant amount of time in the tunnel conducting an EVP session and using an infrared camera to take photographs in the eerily dark location.

While they were standing midway between the top and bottom of the tunnel, Justin spotted something down near the bottom — a glowing ball of bluish-purple colour. At first it just hovered in place, but when they turned off the infrared camera, eliminating any external light, the ball of light started to change. It began to undulate, and its shape altered.

Using the regular camera, Brian started taking pictures, one after another, in rapid succession. Looking at the photos in sequence, it appears the large dark-purple blob is moving quickly up the tunnel toward the investigators before vanishing.

What was it? A bizarre shadow or something else completely? Did it go past them? Through them? Into them? We'll never know for sure, but the photographs certainly make you wonder.

The First Floor

The first floor of Waverly Hills contained some patient and treatment rooms, but its primary purpose was to contain the various things required to maintain a hospital — a small morgue, a salon, a dentist's office, and administration offices. It has since undergone extensive renovation and restoration by the current owners of the hospital, and the first floor currently contains the security office (trespassers are an ongoing problem at Waverly) and a gift shop.

The first floor is not a hotbed of paranormal activity the way some of the other floors appear to be; however, compared to most everywhere else in the world, the first floor is still plenty haunted. In fact, Josh, a Waverly Hills tour guide, told WHIPGhostHunters that there have been a high number of EVPs reported on the first floor.

An EVP is when sounds recorded on electronic devices are interpreted as being the voices of spirits. The voices are frequently not heard by the people recording them at the time. Often only when the recording is played back are EVPs discovered.

In one first-floor treatment room, Josh reports a visitor asking, "Is anybody here?" When they played back the tape of the session, they heard a voice respond clearly, "Well, why are you here?"

The Second Floor

The second floor of Waverly Hills is not well reported upon. This might initially lead you to believe it's not a very active location in the property, but Josh, the same tour guide (who by the very nature of his job spends a significant amount of time all over the hospital), says he's had more paranormal things happen to him in the second-floor cafeteria than in any other room in the building.

One of Waverly Hills' distinguishing features is its solarium. Fresh air and sunlight were believed to be some of the best ways to treat tuberculosis, so Waverly Hills Sanatorium was built so that the entire length of one side is a solarium. While the hospital was operational, that side had a copper mesh over its massive windows in an effort to keep critters out, but still remain open to the Kentucky wind and sunshine. Every day patients would be wheeled out of their rooms and into the solarium to take advantage of these healing elements.

There are a lot of windows in Waverly Hills — in part due to this solarium — so tour guides and visitors to the hospital frequently ask spirits to tap on a window to demonstrate that they are there. One time in the second-floor cafeteria, the spirits were asked to tap a window to say hello. On that occasion something or someone tapped on every single window in the room, moving all the way along one direction, then stopping and tapping them all again in the reverse order. Was this a freaky coincidence, or a spirit trying to make a point?

The Third Floor — Timmy

The spirit of a small child is said to inhabit Waverly Hills. People have taken to calling him "Timmy," and though we were unable to verify that any child named Tim, Timmy, or Timothy was ever a patient at Waverly Hills, perhaps one name is as good as another to this playful spirit. Estimates of his age range from four to seven, but one thing everyone seems to agree on is that he is a mischievous rapscallion.

Timmy's voice has reportedly been caught on EVP, and there are those who believe they've captured his image in photographs, as well. However, the thing Timmy is most famous for is playing ball.

If Timmy *was* a patient at Waverly Hills, there is no question he would have spent most of his time in the children's ward and the rooftop playground on the fifth floor, but most people who have played ball with him have done so on the third floor. Perhaps now that he is unshackled from mortal life and free to run the entire hospital, he's decided he likes the third floor best. Who's to say?

There are dozens of videos on YouTube and paranormal investigation websites purporting to show investigators playing with Timmy. Balls of various sizes and materials roll around or tumble out of shadows down the hall toward a camera.

Unfortunately, most of the videos are shot at night, so they are of questionable quality, with copious shadows and room for doubt. If a ball comes straight out of the darkness toward the camera, for example, how is a viewer to know there wasn't a human foot propelling it from the unseen end of the hall? And in many of the most dramatic videos wind can be heard against the camera's microphone, so perhaps it is merely a breeze, and not a ghost child, moving the ball.

Still, the belief in Timmy and his ball persists, and many people swear that they have seen it move on flat surfaces in interior hallways where there is no wind. It is nice to think that if a child's spirit really is trapped at Waverly Hills, at least it has a lot of investigators stopping by to play with it.

The Third Floor — Mary

"Mary" is the name visitors have given to the other child said to haunt Waverly Hills. According to James Bright's website about Waverly Hills, Mary is often called "Mary Lee" or "Mary Higgs." People believe her to be the spirit of a young woman who died on the third floor. Mary is most known for playing hide-and-seek with visitors to the hospital. There are also those who believe her image was caught in a famous photograph taken in 2006.

The photograph seems to show the image of a young woman standing in a doorway. Her form is transparent. Though you can see what looks like the outline of her body, hair, and face, it is not opaque — parts of the wall behind her are clearly visible. Is this the photograph of a curious young lady checking to see what investigators are doing in her hallway, or is it merely a curious trick of light and shadows? Many are convinced of the former.

A photograph of a spectral image that bears an uncanny resemblance to Mary Lee.

The Third Floor — Man's Best Friend

All hospitals see significant amounts of tragedy, but one assumes that usually stops once they close and stop functioning as hospitals. Not so with Waverly Hills. One of the most heartbreaking stories surrounding this facility is alleged to have happened in the 1990s — at least nine years after it closed. This is the story of a homeless man and his dog.

Waverly Hills had a long period of neglect and was even intentionally damaged by one of its owners. The property owner wanted to build on the site but could not because Waverly Hills had been deemed to have historical importance. During his tenure as caretaker of the property, the owner didn't employ any security, effectively inviting vandals and destruction in the hope that, if the building was damaged enough, it would no longer be protected as a historical site and he could knock it down.

As empty buildings are wont to do, the Hills became the centre of a great many rumours: stories from epic vandalism, to drug users and homeless people, to satanic rituals. The story of the homeless man and his dog occurs within this zeitgeist. While there are many sources for this story, the one we relied upon was the version recounted in Benjamin S. Jeffries's book *Lost in the Darkness*.

Legend says that in the 1990s, an old homeless man and his best friend — a white terrier — made Waverly Hills their home. The man and his dog were happy to have found somewhere safe and sheltered to live, and the new owners were content to let them stay in hopes it would discourage other trespassers who were destroying the historic building. Then one night a group of curious trespassers discovered the man and his dog at the bottom of an elevator shaft. Dead.

Though it may be tempting to assume they merely stumbled into the shaft in the dark, psychics who have visited the site say that's not how it happened. They say the man and his best friend were both murdered — thrown down the elevator shaft and left to die.

Without more information we were unable to verify any details of this story, but Jeffries says that a group of juveniles eventually confessed to this horrible crime. Unfortunately, because of their ages at the time, all the details, including their names, have been kept secret.

Many of those who have visited Waverly Hills believe the ghost of the homeless man continues to haunt the property, perhaps reluctant to give up the last home he and his dog ever had. People have reportedly captured EVPs of a dog barking or howling, heard the dog's collar jingling, and caught glimpses of his owner — an older man wearing a big coat. The pair lurk in hallways and peer out of doorways.

The Fourth Floor

The fourth floor of Waverly Hills is said to be the most haunted of all locations in the hospital, with the possible exception of the body chute. The fourth floor was home to the sickest patients during the hospital's time as a sanatorium, and innumerable drastic surgeries were performed on this floor — including removing up to seven of the patient's ribs, or collapsing a lung by inserting air into the area around it. It is little wonder that the location of so much pain and suffering would be home to more unexplained sounds, voices, shadow people, and apparitions than anywhere else in the hospital.

Big Black

Big Black is possibly the world's largest shadow person — a mass of impenetrable darkness so immense it fills the entire hallway. Imagine being in the hall of a gigantic abandoned hospital when suddenly a dark cloud approaches, swallowing the light from your flashlight. Big Black has been seen in several locations on the fourth floor of Waverly Hills, and in the words of one of the tour guides there, "a large, black shadow ... just settles over the hallway. We call it 'Big Black' and if you see it, you should go the other way."

What would happen if you didn't go the other way? Well, one visitor, who publicly shared his experiences in comments on Mark Ledford's PBase gallery of Waverly Hills, claims to have encountered Big Black in the third-floor operating room. Bill Norman recounted that he felt something brush against his lower back, which then began to burn. When he lifted his shirt, he discovered six long scratches that hadn't been there before. Even more disturbing, when he listened to his voice recorder, he found an EVP of someone, or something, telling them to leave. No one in the room had heard the voice at the time, but his recorder captured it clearly.

That sounds like something worth running from to us!

The Creeper

Sometimes also called "the Crawler," the Creeper is kind of like the "big bad" of the Waverly Hills shadow people. Unlike most shadow people, the Creeper doesn't quite take human form, and it is most often spotted crawling along the walls and ceiling of the fourth and fifth floors. More often than not people mistake the Creeper for just another shadow in an empty building full of shadows. That is until, in the words of Benjamin S. Jeffries, it "stands up and reveals itself as a horrifying, humanoid black mass that escapes … by creeping up the walls."

Based on the various descriptions we've encountered, it is impossible not to imagine the Creeper as something more animal than human. It skitters along impossible surfaces, waiting to pounce, like some grotesque creature in a horror movie. In fact, though most of the shadow people at Waverly Hills (excluding Big Black) are reported to be neutral or benevolent forces, according to an article on the website Exemplore, those encountering the Creeper have described an aura of doom that surrounds it. It is a feeling of malevolence and menace that has to be experienced to be understood.

Some people believe the Creeper may have been a patient who underwent thoracoplasty, the medical procedure that involved cutting out a patient's ribs. Patients who survived this treatment — and there weren't many — lacked the bone structure to stand upright and spent the rest of their lives bent over at the waist.

Is it difficult to imagine that the spirit of a patient who'd undergone such pain and suffering might remain, in a twisted form, trapped on the floor of the hospital where it happened? And if that truly is the the Creeper's origin, is it any wonder that it would exude a dark and menacing aura?

Unnamed Shadow People

Big Black and the Creeper are not the only shadow people to inhabit the fourth floor, and certainly not the only ones on the property. It seems as though spotting shadow people meandering about the grounds and all floors of the hospital is actually very common.

For the most part they appear to be oblivious to their human visitors — as in this story told by paranormal investigator Becky Ray:

> It's not like one or two, these "people" are everywhere in this building. They are like shadows that pass up and down the hallways, in and out of doorways, look out of windows, and it is just like someone is there. They actually move and break the moonlight. I'd never seen anything like it. At one point, they were literally all around us.

Still, sometimes the shadow people do take notice of people trespassing on their property. Early one morning, at about 4 a.m., a small tour group went up to the fourth floor of the Hills. As soon as they entered the floor, one of the group, let's call him "Jamie," felt uneasy. What's more, his nostrils were assailed with the overwhelming scent of roses — an odour that grew stronger and stronger with every step he took onto the ward.

While his friends went into an operating room, Jamie kept his back pressed against the wall, his eyes focused on the solarium that spans the entire front of the building. Suddenly, as though out of nowhere, a dark shadowy figure began to walk around in the solarium.

Jamie dashed into the operating room to tell his friends, but everyone assumed he was just seeing things … right up until they returned to the hall, and they all saw the apparition.

The shadow stood at the end of the hall, exactly where the little tour group had been when they'd first entered the ward. The shadow and the tour group stared at one another in silence for a very long time. Then, as though at some signal no one else was aware of, the shadow began to float down the hall toward them, its arms, as Jamie explained, "moving like a distorted power walk." Its darkness was so dense that it swallowed the light coming in from doorways and the outdoors. It kept coming and coming.

Finally, the brave tour guide stepped between the entity and the little group of visitors. He told the spirit they didn't mean any harm and would leave if it gave them a sign. The shadow was only two doors away from the little group when, as suddenly as it had appeared, it vanished again.

Locked In

Tour guides at Waverly Hills like to tell the story of two young would-be vandals — this story has also been shared both on the Bedford Paranormal website and in Benjamin S. Jeffries's book *Lost in the Darkness*. The pair allegedly broke into the hospital armed with an axe and some spray paint. It would seem their intent was to leave their mark on the building, but apparently the spirits who reside there had other plans.

The security guard was alerted to the intruders' presence when he heard screams and cries for help echoing through the empty halls. He tracked down the source and found the two boys trapped on the fourth floor in a great deal of distress. One was trying to squeeze through a small window in the door to the staircase, and the other was chopping at the door with his axe.

"They are all around us!" they screamed. "The door is stuck! Get us out of here!"

The security guard tried the door to let the trespassers out, and it opened without any resistance — it hadn't been locked at all, but the boys who'd intended the hospital harm hadn't been able to open it even with the aid of an axe.

What had driven them to such desperation that they were trying to climb through windows and chop through the door with an axe? What was all around them?

No one knows except the boys, and they aren't talking. Still, given Becky Ray's report about being surrounded by shadow people, one has to wonder if maybe that's what the boys saw. Perhaps the spirits objected to the boys' intentions toward the hospital and wanted to scare them away. I suppose we'll never know, but it does make you think, doesn't it?

The Fifth Floor

The fifth floor of Waverly Hills is possibly the most surreal. In addition to containing rooms for patients (specifically those being treated for TB with sunlight), it also contains something not often seen inside a hospital — a swing set.

Tuberculosis isn't selective about those it affects, so Waverly Hills was home to patients of all ages, including the very young. In *Lost in the Darkness*, Benjamin S. Jeffries reports on how the staff dealt with the Hills' younger guests. In an attempt to provide them some relief from what must have been an incredibly depressing place to grow up (even without taking the effects of TB into account), the staff set up a swing set on the rooftop. During the day the kids were encouraged to play on it, out in the sunlight and fresh air — both of which were thought to be effective treatments for tuberculosis. It must have provided a lift for their spirits as well as an improvement in their physical health. Perhaps this explains the numerous childlike spirits that are said to inhabit the rooftop playground. Investigators and visitors have reported hearing childlike giggling, snatches of nursery rhymes, and the sounds of unseen children playing.

Room 502

By far the most notorious room at Waverly Hills Sanatorium is room 502.

Allegedly, this is the room where a young nurse's body was found hanged in 1928. There are at least three different stories about how her body got there, but all of them have to do with her being pregnant out of wedlock. Nowadays this happens all the time and is more or less accepted within North American society. In 1928, though, not so much. Legend says that the nurse hanged herself either out of shame at her situation or because she knew her friends and family would ostracize her if they were to find out.

Variations on this legend, however, become ever more bloody and tragic. Some stories say the nurse first gave herself an abortion before she hanged herself. Others claim the father of her child, a married doctor at the hospital, tried to abort the fetus but botched the job, and she died on the operating table. According to that story, he then staged it to look like a suicide to protect his reputation, both personal and professional.

There are no official records of a suicide in that room, but, even so, people believe an unearthly presence inhabits it. According to the Prairie Ghosts website, visitors to the room frequently report feeling ill. Their symptoms range from slight nausea to violent, uncontrollable vomiting. People have also reported seeing a figure draped in white, shadow people moving across the windows and blocking light as they pass, and disembodied voices demanding that they "Get out!"

At Waverly Hills Sanatorium urban legend and reality are woven together so seamlessly that it is difficult, if not impossible, to see where one ends and the other begins. The current owners offer tours of the building, both historical and paranormal, so while its legend continues to grow from the addition of new visitors' personal experiences to the milieu, so, too, do the number of skeptics who believe it to just be an eerie building with a sad history. But while it is impossible to prove many of the stories that surround Waverly Hills, it's equally impossible to disprove the belief of some that it is one of the most haunted locations in the world.

MASSACHUSETTS

Danvers State Hospital: The Birthplace of the Lobotomy

Danvers

The Danvers State Hospital is located on top of a hill in Danvers, Massachusetts. What you need to know about Danvers, Massachusetts, though, is that before it was called Danvers, the town went by another name — Salem. Yes, that Salem. Not only was this village where the Salem witch trials took place, but the judge who presided over those trials, John Hathorne, used to live on the same hill where the hospital was later built.

Besides its notorious location, the hospital in Danvers has an unnerving history of performing controversial and experimental procedures, and a reputation for poor treatment of patients. In fact, it is known as the birthplace of the lobotomy.

Since the hospital closed in 1992, its legend has only grown. Stories abound about urban explorers and paranormal investigators feeling suddenly ill, or being overcome with feelings of despair when they venture into certain parts of the building. Doors open and close on their own, footsteps have been heard in empty rooms and stairways, and full-body apparitions of former patients have even been spotted wandering and screaming through the empty hallways.

Metropolitan State Hospital: Murder and Empathy

Waltham

Once one of the largest modern-equipped facilities of its type in the state, the Metropolitan State Hospital, a hospital for the mentally ill, closed its doors in 1992. Having fallen into disrepair while sitting vacant for many years, most of the buildings on the complex were demolished in 2009.

The only two things remaining from the site's history are the abandoned and boarded-up Dr. William McLaughlin Administration Building, which is a foreboding stately Colonial Revival building from 1927, and a cemetery maintained by the Commonwealth of Massachusetts.

Originally opened in 1930, the nearly five-hundred-acre property has been used for multiple purposes over the years, including a school for juvenile offenders, an operational farm, a haunted house to raise money for charity, and the site of a new apartment complex.

The most likely source for the paranormal activity on this site, however, stems back to the torments experienced by the residents of this hospital, those who left their tortured spirits behind. There are also more than 350 patients who were buried in paupers' graves on the grounds, with nothing more than a stone to mark their religion and their number.

One of the non-paranormal yet dark stories that the hospital is known for is the murderous act of a patient by the name of Melvin W. Wilson. Wilson murdered and dismembered a patient named Anne Marie Davee with a hatchet, and he buried several pieces of her body in different locations on the sprawling hospital grounds. Wilson allegedly kept seven of his victim's teeth as a sort of souvenir, but they were discovered by employees at the hospital. The incident itself was apparently brushed under the rug until a local senator, nearly two years later, led an investigation into allegations of negligence at the hospital that uncovered this travesty.

In the *Encyclopedia of Haunted Places*, Jeff Belanger reports that while the hospital was still in operation, staff reported various different paranormal episodes, including the uncanny sight of strange shadowy figures moving down hallways, entering and exiting rooms, and passing through the walls.

Staff had also reported hearing the shrill call of disembodied screams coming from locations where, decades earlier, electroshock therapy had been used on patients. The belief is that the staff was hearing echoes of the angst and pain from patients who had long since passed away. Perhaps even more startling are reports of flashing lights from those same areas, flashes that are thought to be representative of the shock treatments used.

The New England Center for the Advancement of Paranormal Science (also known as Para-Boston) specializes in the research and investigation of claims of paranormal activity throughout the State of Massachusetts as well as east central New England. Para-Boston wrote a detailed report about this location in an April 2013 article on its website.

Among the incidents documented at the hospital are voices heard to be engaged in conversation in rooms and hallways where there is nobody present, workers being grabbed and touched by unseen hands while moving through the tunnels that linked the various site buildings, and heavy doors slamming shut violently despite the absence of wind or open windows.

In 2011, reports of a "glowing blue" woman were made by more than a dozen different residents. The woman was spotted near a sidewalk up the road from the Main Administrative Building. Police actually investigated, searching for a woman described to be gardening beside the sidewalk, but despite the many reports, no woman matching her description could be found. Could this ghost be the spirit of Anne Marie Davee, wandering about the grounds, searching for the parts of her body that were buried by her murderer?

Among the most disturbing of reported incidents at the old Metropolitan State Hospital (recounted in Jeff Belanger's *Encyclopedia of Haunted Places*) are the ones made by those who feel as if they are being watched and are overcome by a flood of emotions while walking the beautiful and scenic grounds. Some report feeling physically ill, only to return to normal almost immediately after leaving the area. But while on the grounds, they are consumed by feelings of neglect and rejection — an empathetic reaction, perhaps, to the spirits that linger on the grounds. A few have even shared mental images that came with these powerful emotions, describing horrific procedures and practices enacted upon the former patients.

NEW JERSEY

Overbrook Asylum for the Insane: Frozen to Death

Cedar Grove

Originally built to help relieve overcrowding at Greystone Park, the Essex County Hospital, most frequently called the Overbrook Asylum for the Insane, was built in 1872. Hospitals, by their very nature, are sites for a multitude of minor tragedies. In addition to those expected tragedies, in December of 1917 the heating and electrical plant for Overbrook failed, so there was no heat or light inside the hospital. A cold snap in the weeks that followed led to frostbite for thirty-two patients, and twenty-four patients had died from the cold by the time heat and power were properly restored.

The hospital was shut down in 2007, and the remaining buildings are frequently patrolled by law enforcement in an effort to keep ghost hunters and urban explorers from within its walls. Even so, photographs, videos, and stories of Overbrook abound on the internet, and it has been visited (with permission) by several television crews who specialize in discovering and documenting paranormal activity.

Visitors to the hospital and its grounds have reported seeing bizarrely distorted shadows, orbs, and disembodied voices. Chuck Palahniuk filmed the movie adaptation of his novel *Choke* at Overbrook Asylum, and claimed there was one teamster who wouldn't leave his truck after repeatedly seeing a grey-haired woman in a white cap and uniform. Apparently the figure would disappear midway down a hall or into dead-end rooms.

John Edmunds shared some of the video he shot at Overbrook on YouTube. He has footage of what he called "the scariest four legged freak" wandering in the abandoned halls of the empty asylum. In the video "Overbrook Insane Asylum Essex County Hospital Scary Sighting," it looks much like a person walking on all fours, so while we hesitate to call it supernatural, it would admittedly be a discomforting thing to see if you weren't expecting it.

Others have claimed to see white masses that resembled people looking out the windows and to hear unexplainable voices. It has been pointed out by skeptics in the YouTube video, "Essex County Overbrook Asylum," by user cnb23, that the large hospital is so frequently broken into by vandals, ghost hunters, and urban explorers that it's impossible to know if you're the only person inside. So are people witnessing spirits or just other curious trespassers? We don't know for sure.

Greystone Park Psychiatric Hospital: Gravestone

Morris Plains

Greystone Park Psychiatric Hospital is a mammoth building. In fact, it had the largest footprint of any single building in the United States right up until the Pentagon was built in 1943. Originally the building had a name as big as its footprint — New Jersey State Lunatic Asylum at Morristown — but in 1924 it was renamed Greystone Park. The hospital is most affectionately known as "Gravestone."

Gravestone is the name given to the facility by one of its most famous patients, folksinger Woody Guthrie. Back in the days of these incredibly huge mental hospitals, patients were frequently admitted for things we would not consider mental illnesses today. Guthrie is a perfect example of that — he lived at Greystone from 1956 to 1961 because he was afflicted with Huntington's disease. Another famous musician, Bob Dylan, also spent some time there.

As with many of the hospitals in this book, while Greystone Park was open, rumours of patient mistreatment and abuse surrounded it like a fog. Since its closure in 2003 these rumours have been replaced with stories of hauntings and spirits. In *Lost in the Darkness* Benjamin S. Jeffries discusses the whispered stories about light anomalies, mysterious door and window openings and closings, and even sightings of the faces of former patients looking out the windows forlornly.

Paranormal romance author Denise K. Rago, who lives near Greystone, claims that groundsworkers have reported feeling watched while they were there. Scott Haefner says he saw a full-body apparition in the old shower area in the basement when he visited. While he was on site photographing the abandoned building, he watched as a planter with fake flowers slowly "twisted back and forth as if being influenced by looming spirits" even though there was no discernible breeze and the windows were all boarded up.

NEW YORK

Riverside Hospital: Typhoid Mary

North Brother Island

"Typhoid Mary" is a term often used to refer to the origin of an illness outbreak. For example, if someone comes into your office coughing on Tuesday, and by Friday everyone who works with her is sick, you might call her Typhoid Mary. But the phrase "Typhoid Mary" originated with a real person. Mary Mallon, the first person to ever be called Typhoid Mary, was also the first person in the United States to be identified as an asymptomatic carrier of typhoid fever. Though Mary was immune to the disease and didn't exhibit any symptoms of it, she was still able to infect other people. Once they identified her as the source of several typhoid outbreaks, authorities attempted to talk Mary out of continuing to work as a cook in order to minimize the risk she posed, but she refused. Typhoid is mostly spread through fecal-oral transmission, so if Mary wasn't handling people's food, she would be less likely to infect them. Mary infected at least fifty-three people (three of whom died) and, in order to protect the public, she was quarantined in the Riverside Hospital until her death many years later.

The hospital, and in fact the entire island, is widely thought to be haunted, but the specific form of the haunting is difficult to pin down, perhaps because the island has been largely abandoned for decades. That's all about to change, however, as there are plans to open it to the public. Who knows what stories will begin to trickle out once more people are able to visit!

Rolling Hills Asylum: A Hotbed of Activity

East Bethany

From the outside, the Rolling Hills Asylum is a picturesque red brick building, with its big main door set between two wings that jut out at right angles to either side. It's lovely, and it looks like a fantastic place to wander through. You might even want to have a picnic right out on the front lawn — however, your picnic would unlikely be as peaceful as first appearances might imply because the Rolling Hills Asylum is said to be a hotbed of paranormal activity.

Rolling Hills opened as the Genesee County Poor Farm in 1827 with the noble intention of housing those in need, like orphans, widows, and the homeless. It was a large farm — two hundred acres of property — and the original building wasn't exactly small either at 53,000 square feet.

Running an institution of this size is not cheap, however, so despite the good intentions that inspired its creation, eventually in order to make

Rolling Hills Asylum.

ends meet Rolling Hills expanded the range of people it took in. Soon criminals and the insane joined the ranks of those too poor or weak to take care of themselves, all of them living next door to one another.

During an interview for the *Ghost Adventures* television show, which is about a trio of ghost hunters who travel the world investigating haunted properties, paranormal investigator Stacey Jones said, "If you were a mother with children, you were put on the same floor with drunkards or pedophiles." Do we dare imagine what that living situation must have been like? With the criminally insane living under the very same roof as their perfect victims? It must have been a perpetrator's paradise, and a hell for those who were only at the poor farm in the first place because they were unable to fend for themselves.

After the Civil War, investigators did studies on the various poor farms and, according to Stacey Jones, the poor farm that eventually became Rolling Hills was considered the worst in the state with regards to how those within its walls were treated. Hardly surprising, really. You'd have to work pretty hard to provide worse care to the weakest members of society than to house them with criminals.

Once it ceased to function as a poor farm, the Genesee County Infirmary was built on the grounds. That hospital had a long lifespan, including a stint as a tuberculosis sanatorium, before eventually becoming a nursing home.

With approximately seventeen hundred people buried on the property, a tumultuous history that included selling children as labourers, and rumours of witchcraft and magic spells being cast on the grounds, is it any wonder this is known as one of the most active paranormal sites in the United States?

The Electrical Substation

There is an electrical substation directly across the street from Rolling Hills Asylum. Skeptics believe it is possible that some of the credit for the unexplained noises, sightings, and equipment readings belongs to this substation. They think electromagnetic interference from the substation can explain many of the phenomena experienced at Rolling Hills. However, while filming the ghost hunting show *Ghost Asylum*, one investigator reported that once he moved about twenty feet away from the station, his equipment stopped registering any EMF (electromagnetic frequencies) from the station. If that's the case, is it really fair to dismiss unexplained activity as electromagnetic interference?

Some have another theory. They believe that the substation acts as a sort of battery, fuelling the spirits that remain at Rolling Hills. Current owner Sharon Coyle said, "We have a power grid across the street, which I think feeds a lot of the activity.... I really believe that that's, like, a food source, if you will. An energy source." If Sharon is correct, then the power station is the cause of some of the paranormal activity experienced at the Hills, but not in the way skeptics would have you believe.

Screaming Woman

One of the most frequently experienced phenomena at the Rolling Hills is that of the screaming woman. At any time of the day or night, a blood-curdling scream might come out of nowhere to assault your eardrums. It echoes through the hallways and is so loud that it has even been heard outside the building. There is no way to predict when it will happen, but the sound has been caught on tape and is very disturbing to hear.

Don't Touch Me!

Nurse Emmie Altworth is one of the more malevolent spirits said to reside at Rolling Hills. Not only does Nurse Emmie have a reputation for having been a downright unpleasant woman — violent and abusive — she is also alleged to have dabbled in black magic and belonged to a satanic coven.

Emmie's presence is often felt around the grounds, especially in her old room. Tucked back in a far corner of the top floor, at the end of a narrow, poorly lit hallway, her room is lonely and unnerving. Witness Suzie Yencer explained, "Whenever you come into Emmie's room … you get that heavy — it's just, it's unsettling." Suzie also reported that men are often groped by an unseen entity in Emmie's old room.

The satanic coven Emmie was once a part of is still active and practising. In fact, a decade or so ago the coven broke into Rolling Hills. In the dead of night they snuck in and performed a ritual just down the hallway from Emmie's room. When the caretakers discovered the ritual site, there were candles, drawn circles, and feathers on the walls.

What kind of vile ritual were they performing? What were they trying to accomplish with their black magic? It's difficult to believe that it was coincidence that they performed their dark rites just down the hall from where the nurse used to live and is known to haunt. Was Emmie somehow a ghostly participant?

The male counterpart to Emmie at Rolling Hills, especially in the realm of unwanted touching, is Raymond. Raymond is almost as well known as Roy, whom you'll read about in a moment, but where Roy is known for being friendly and sympathetic, Raymond is the exact opposite.

In *Lost in the Darkness*, Benjamin S. Jeffries says the rumour is that Raymond was once a patient at Rolling Hills, and during his time there he molested some of the little girls who were unfortunate enough to share a roof with him. It would seem that death didn't improve Raymond's temperament; women who've ventured down into the tunnels and basement that were Raymond's lair in life have reported being groped and attacked by someone they couldn't see. Is Raymond still haunting these grounds, molesting people who can't fight back? It's possible. And the attacks extend beyond sexual touching into the realm of violent outbursts — Marlena Treat, for example, had a piece of wood thrown at her by an unseen assailant in one of the underground tunnels. Who threw it? No one can say for sure that it was Raymond, but given the location of the attack he seems a likely suspect.

Roy Crouse

The most beloved, and probably the most well-known ghostly resident of Rolling Hills Asylum is Roy Crouse. Born in 1890, Roy was afflicted with gigantism, which is a medical condition that, just as it sounds, results in extensive growth. People with gigantism grow to be anywhere from seven to nearly nine feet tall (the tallest man ever, Robert Wadlow, was eight feet eleven inches). Roy's height did not rival Robert Wadlow, but his peak height was said to be over seven feet tall, far taller than most men.

Roy's parents left him at the Genesee County Poor Farm when he was only twelve years old, presumably because society (and his family) had a difficult time accepting his unusual size and appearance. Despite how devastating it must have been for a twelve-year-old boy to be abandoned in a place like the Genesee County Poor Farm, Roy is said to have made himself a comfortable life there. Often referred to as a "gentle giant," he spent a lot of time in the library reading everything he could get his hands on, and he even accumulated a substantial library of his own. He also became enamoured with music, especially classical music. He was comfortable there, and he lived there his entire life until he died at the age of sixty-two. In fact, there are those who say Roy remains there even now.

A huge shadow in the shape of a person has been photographed at Rolling Hills several times. Is this Roy? This shadow is most often spotted in what has become known as "Shadow Person Hallway" in the second-floor men's ward. Dozens of shadow people have been seen in this location, but the one said to be Roy stands out because of its size.

When the television show *Ghost Hunters* filmed at Rolling Hills, they sealed up Shadow Person Hallway to prevent any drafts or natural disturbances and set up a laser grid over it. Then they filled the hall with dense fog that they allowed to settle to the ground. The result is a visual representation of air currents in the area. They filmed for over ten minutes without seeing anything unusual. Then, after they specifically called Roy and asked him to walk through the fog, reassuring him that it wouldn't hurt him, they saw something. An odd-looking energy surge extends into the grid and then suddenly disappears in a burst, somewhat like a balloon popping. Was that Roy? Did he come take a look before deciding he didn't want to be there anymore?

In death Roy is as beloved as he was in life, and every year the current owners of Rolling Hills Asylum actually celebrate his birthday with cake in the room that used to be his. In April 2015 some investigators went to Nurse Emmie's room with cake to celebrate her birthday, and during their visit it appeared that some unseen entity was intelligently interacting with their equipment (lighting up lights when prompted and in response to questions). But where Nurse Emmie has a reputation for being vile and mean-spirited, this entity was friendly and pleasant. In fact, the investigators believed it was Roy, rather than Emmie, who was communicating with them.

Perhaps he didn't understand the party wasn't for him, or perhaps he didn't care. After all, birthday cake is birthday cake, right?

The Christmas Room

If Raymond really was a patient who molested children at Rolling Hills Asylum, the Christmas Room is a chilling reminder of the sheer number of potential victims he had easy access to. Because this facility was used to house everyone from orphans to the criminally insane, a great number of children lived here — so many, in fact, that the Christmas Room was created in an attempt to cheer them up in what must have been a very dismal place to spend one's childhood.

In this room it's like Christmas every day — there's a decorated tree, plenty of toys, garland, and even stockings hung by a fake fireplace, waiting for Santa Claus to come fill them. In its time this must have been a joyful place filled with the laughter of children, but now there is something uncanny and off-putting about it.

The current owners of Rolling Hills Asylum come to this room and read stories to the ghosts of children who linger here, and reportedly those same spirits respond to the stories through EVP. It would seem the spirits like to play, as well, because when toy cars are placed on the ground in this room, they will sometimes move a little bit — under the control of a ghostly hand, perhaps?

There are some who believe the Christmas Room is inhabited by something darker than the spirits of children, something demonic. The theory is that not many people would knowingly open themselves up to demonic influence, but most people would want to comfort and console a lost child if they discovered one, so a demon clever enough to pretend to be a child might find a much more receptive audience or vessel than one who revealed its true nature. So what really inhabits this room? Is it the ghosts of children, a demonic lure, or something else entirely?

The Morgue

There is no room at Rolling Hills more different from the Christmas Room than the morgue. The Christmas Room was intended to give children comfort and a place to play, but the morgue is coldly practical and, one hopes, not often frequented by youngsters.

A morgue is a uncomfortable place to be at the best of times but the morgue at Rolling Hills is even more so than a usual morgue. Stories abound about people feeling ill just from proximity to the table there. This seems especially to afflict people who work in the medical field although no one seems to have a theory as to why. When the ghost hunters from *Ghost Asylum* investigated Rolling Hills, one of them, Porter, lay down on the slab and immediately felt unwell. "This feels really weird. It almost feels like vertigo," he said. "As soon as I lay down on the slab I felt this freaky sensation all through my bod. The room was spinnin'. My stomach was churnin'. I've never felt anything this crazy before."

When Chasey Ray replaced Porter on the table, he immediately felt dizzy, as well, and started to ask for help, saying that something was going wrong in the morgue — an attempt to get the attention of any nearby spirits. The current owners have a suit hanging from the ceiling in the morgue, and right away it began to spin in place, as though stirred by a strong breeze or an unseen hand. The investigators reported that there were no drafts or breezes, though, so what was causing the suit to move?

OHIO

The Ridges: Etched in Stone

Athens

The hospital now known as the Ridges had nine different official names between when it opened in 1874 as Athens Lunatic Asylum and when it closed in 1993.

The sad story of Margaret Schilling begins on December 1, 1978, when the hospital was called the Athens Mental Health Center. According to Dinah Williams's book *Abandoned Insane Asylums*, Margaret Schilling, a patient at the facility, disappeared in the middle of winter. Though search parties were formed and the hospital and grounds searched, no one was able to locate her, and eventually the search was called off. Weeks later a janitor went up into the attic and made a shocking discovery — Margaret's body.

The stories say Margaret used to love to play hide-and-seek — had she been hiding up there from those looking for her, or had she become lost and been unable to find her way out of the attic? No one would ever know for sure. However, when her body was removed from the freezing cold attic, a detailed outline of it remained on the stone floor. It's so detailed, in fact, that the style of her hair and even some of the folds

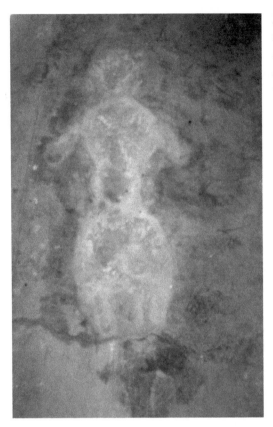

No matter how many times the floor was cleaned, a stain showing the outline of Margaret Schilling's body remained.

of her clothes can be seen. No matter how many times the floor was cleaned, the outline remained.

In an article in the *Journal of Forensic Sciences*, Carolyn Zimmermann discusses the tests that have since been done on the stain. According to Zimmermann, tests prove that, though it seems that at some point someone used chemicals that etched the outline deeper into the floor, the outline was definitely formed by human remains.

Some people believe that Margaret haunts the hospital. This is sad, if true, but given that the outline of her earthly form remains, it seems only appropriate that her spirit would, too.

PENNSYLVANIA

Private Residence: A Doctor in the Haunted House

Mechanics Grove

It has not been uncommon, particularly in the past, for doctors to conduct business out of their homes. It also sometimes happens that a doctor is charged with malpractice. In the case of this particular story from a 1935 edition of the *Gettysburg Times*, a mystery is solved, a doctor is arrested, and locals continue to decry the house where he performed his evil acts as haunted.

DOCTOR'S ARREST JUST WHAT THEY EXPECTED

Mechanics Grove, April 20 (AP) — The "haunted house" of the Susquehanna River Hills has come to the very end villagers predicted for it.

That's why they seldom looked up from their plowing, though police cars roared up to the ramshackle farm of Dr. H.E. Zimmerly and reporters and cameramen phoned frantically from the crossroads grocery store.

Lifelong residents of Mechanics Grove shrugged or shook their heads after state police and county detectives broke into the house the other day and arrested the village doctor. They were not surprised, they said, when a young girl was carried from the house to an ambulance.

Show Little Interest
They showed little interest in the charges that Dr. Zimmerly performed illegal operations and that he had violated the narcotic laws. They pointed to the high board fence he erected on the one end of his lot; so high that it shut off the view of the second-storey windows of his neighbor's dwelling.

They've wondered about the Zimmerly house, they said, regarding their strange neighbor. There were some who recalled that "he treated the poor and never took pay for them." But others insisted the house is "haunted," and whispered about cries they've heard in the night, and dim lights burning "at all hours."

Remember His History

They said Dr. Zimmerly had come there "over fifteen years ago." They remembered the day his wife left him, with their daughter. They remembered, too, how he built a large tile garage in front of his property and planned to operate a gasoline service station. But he never opened the place. And he seldom was seen in the faded yellow barn adjoining the garage.

Neighbors told state police and the district attorney's staff that "half a dozen or more" cars stopped at the Zimmerly place every night. Most of them came out of the main road to Baltimore. Many of the visitors were women.

Not Active in Village

Zimmerly seldom took part in affairs of the village nor mingled with his neighbors. So he lived from day to day. Dick Parker, heavyset handyman, seemed to be his only consistent companion.

Neighbors said they knew Parker would be arrested the day Zimmerly was. "Whatever was the Doc's was Dick's," is the way they put it.

Over the hills in Lancaster, the two cronies were locked up, while Elsie Miller, the Rising Sun, Maryland, girl the police found in the "haunted house," was removed to a hospital and detectives were told to "find Gladys Lawson," who also was a patient there.

Still Haunted House

There were stories that Mrs. Lawson was buried on the farm after she underwent an operation in the little front room upstairs. There were whisperings that "others may be buried there."

But Mechanics Grove has little to say about rumors, little to say for or against the accused village doctor or his "handy man," but they know the "house is haunted."

Dixmont State Hospital: Guarding the Morgue

Pittsburgh

Originally known as the Department of the Insane in the Western Pennsylvania Hospital of Pittsburgh, this hospital, which was built upon a campus that spanned more than four hundred acres, was once considered state of the art and extremely self-sufficient. It was built partially in response to need. After the Western Pennsylvania Hospital of Pittsburgh's first year of operation in 1853, it became clear to legislatures that the twenty-six beds were nowhere close to sufficient to meet the needs of the much larger number of patients in local jails and almshouses — places of residence for the poor, the old, and the distressed.

Construction on the site began in 1859 and Dixmont opened its doors in 1862 with 113 patients. By the turn of the century, the hospital's multiple buildings housed anywhere between twelve hundred and fifteen hundred patients.

Like so many similar institutions, Dixmont became severely overcrowded. It was a time before the diagnosis of post-traumatic stress disorder, but soldiers in need of care returned from the First World War in the 1920s, filling hospitals. By the Great Depression, when significant financial difficulties plagued the institution, Dixmont couldn't afford to pay staff anything more than room and board. The Pennsylvania Department of Welfare eventually stepped in, and Dixmont became a state-owned hospital by 1946. Shortly after, previously decried procedures involving the use of restraints, electroshock therapy, and lobotomies began. By the mid-1970s the financial situation at Dixmont had become even worse, and as support and interest from the state continued to wane, it closed in 1984 and was demolished in 2006.

Among the many spirits and entities said to have haunted the Dixmont State Hospital was the ghost of a man reported to be guarding the morgue. Allegedly, the man stood guard in this particular part of the hospital, suddenly appearing and frightening away intruders. One wonders if this might be the spirit of one of the dedicated staff members who remained at the hospital throughout its declining years, protective of the patients and recently deceased inmates, and leery of the intrusion of the state, which ultimately played a role in the institution's demise.

Pennhurst Asylum: Attractions and Horrific Histories

Pennhurst

In Pennhurst, Pennsylvania, there exists an asylum that is both the shame and the pride — albeit a particularly dark and demented one — of the state.

Having first opened its doors in November 1908, Pennhurst Asylum immediately became overcrowded after succumbing to pressures to admit not only the mentally and physically handicapped, but also criminals, orphans, and immigrants. Five years after the asylum opened, a Commission for the Care of the Feeble-Minded was appointed. The Commission went on to declare that those persons with disabilities were "unfit for citizenship" and posed a menace to the peace of society in general. Patients were also lumped into different group categories; under such categories as "mental prowess," an inmate could be declared "insane" or "imbecile."

More than ten thousand patients went through this facility, and many of them were exposed to an ongoing regimen of mental, physical, and sexual abuse — often at such atrocious extremes that some even died from the maltreatment.

Considered one of the most striking examples of the maltreatment of patients, a 1972 *Pottstown Mercury* newspaper article labelled Pennhurst

"The Shame of Pennsylvania," calling the asylum a "vast junkyard of wasted humans."

The Pennhurst Paranormal Association, which offers both public and private paranormal investigations of the asylum, has conducted many large-scale investigations of their own over the years. Some of the phenomena they have recorded include disembodied voices uttering things such as "we're upset," "why'd you come here," "go away," and "I'll kill you."

Within the Quaker Building are the shadowy manifestations of what appears to be a young girl with long black hair, long dangling arms, and a severely hunched posture. Investigators in this building were both scratched and shoved by unseen hands, and a medium has reported a decidedly dark and powerful evil presence in the building. According to the medium, this could only be a demonic force or perhaps the spiritual manifestation of a truly evil person.

In the Limerick Building the spectral appearance of a woman wearing an old-fashioned nurse's uniform was observed by three different individuals. Multiple EVPs have also been recorded, revealing the presence of some odd and otherworldly entities.

Loud echoing voices can be heard coming from the Philadelphia Building. This despite the fact that, at the time, investigators completely surrounded the building before moving in, ensuring that no human inside could have escaped the building without being detected.

The property is currently in the hands of private owners who operate a popular haunted-house attraction on the site, drawing from the location's dark and disturbing past. Certain controversy exists regarding this use of the space, as some believe that the dramatized horrors solely for entertainment purposes is disrespectful of the patients and inmates who suffered the indignity and brutality that was once common there.

One thing we know for certain is that people continue to be fascinated by both mortality and history. The attraction at Pennhurst allows exploration of both in a unique and fascinating way, and an otherwise abandoned historic site is being used to stimulate tourism and the local economy.

Pennhurst Asylum hosts tours of the hospital, focusing on historic artifacts, ghostly legends, and chillingly fun terror.

The following are the various attractions available at Pennhurst Asylum according to its website:

> *Pennhurst Attractions*: This tour includes a hospital-themed haunted walk through the Pennhurst Asylum with a focus on the artifacts and items that were part of the original State School.

> *The Dungeon of Lost Souls*: This walk-through features a labyrinth of old cells and a series of experiments that have gone horribly wrong.

> *The Tunnel Terror*: This walk goes through a nine-hundred-foot tunnel underneath the grounds of the State School.

> *Ghost Hunt*: A self-guided tour of the Mayflower Building, which is reportedly among the most actively haunted locations on the site. Visitors are armed only with a flashlight as they wander through the dorm.

One final thought on this interesting attraction is that it not only allows people to experience a unique and stimulating thrill, but it also ensures that those who are curious to go on ghost hunts don't end up wandering through dangerous asbestos-filled buildings in order to experience that frightening sensation. At this attraction, people are safe from the real-life hazards that come with exploring abandoned sites.

Or are they?

WEST VIRGINIA

Trans-Allegheny Lunatic Asylum: Tragic Separation

Weston

The stories say that once you were admitted to the Trans-Allegheny Lunatic Asylum, you never got out again — at least not alive. Originally called the Weston State Hospital, the institution now known as the Trans-Allegheny Lunatic Asylum was established in 1858. It took over twenty years to build, possibly because its construction was happening at the same time as the American Civil War. Encompassing over half a million square feet, this hospital is the second largest hand-cut stone building in the world — smaller only than the Moscow Kremlin.

The hospital was originally intended to house a maximum of 250 patients but in the 1950s it reportedly had over 2,400 of them. Nearly ten times its intended occupancy! The conditions in such an overcrowded hospital must have been abhorrent. Especially when you consider the quality of those patients. This hospital, much like Rolling Hills Asylum, housed the criminally insane alongside orphans. The records do show attempts to separate high- and low-risk patients from one another, and also to segregate by gender. But still, what a mix it must have been to have people forcibly admitted for insanity or criminal activity under the same roof as those institutionalized for reasons ranging from homosexuality, to addiction, to homelessness, and to simple abandonment. Even Charles Manson spent a short amount of time incarcerated here.

The legends say that those who were admitted to the Trans-Allegheny Lunatic Asylum never got out again.

Common treatments during the time this hospital was operational included electroshock therapy and lobotomies, but the lobotomies performed at Weston State Hospital were reportedly even more brutal than average. Apparently instead of using anaesthesia, doctors used electroshock therapy to shock patients to unconsciousness (or near unconsciousness). Then a frontal lobotomy was performed with the use of tools as primitive as an ice pick. Individually, lobotomies and old-fashioned electroshock therapy were traumatic experiences, but combining them into one procedure seems especially brutal.

The hospital was closed in 1994, but was purchased in 2007 by Joe Jordan in a public auction. Joe changed the facility's name back to the original Trans-Allegheny Lunatic Asylum and now offers historic and paranormal tours of the property.

Lilly

Perhaps the most heartbreakingly tragic story to emerge from the shadows of the Trans-Allegheny Lunatic Asylum is that of Lilly.

The sounds of children running, playing, and giggling have been reported in several locations within the hospital, but Lilly, the spirit of a young girl, seems to stick around the Civil War section. Reportedly this lonely little thing will take unattended candy out of its wrapper, or hold people's hands as they walk through the hospital.

One of the most dramatic stories around Lilly comes from Weston local Shelley Bailey, as told in a "Real Hauntings Paranormal Documentary" available on YouTube. Shelley was leading a tour through the Civil War section of the hospital. One of the women on her tour arrived prepared to encounter Lilly — she had a box of Cracker Jack and a ball. Inside one of the rooms, the woman set the box of candy upright on the edge of the sink. Untouched by anyone in the room, the box reportedly fell over, still on the edge of the sink, and began to spin in a circle. Then it fell into the sink's basin. Though Shelley and the other people on her tour could no longer see the box they could hear "the box fumbling around as if someone was trying to open" it. Soon after, even though the box hadn't been opened, they could hear the sound of chewing and one of the visitors recorded an EVP of a voice saying, "Thank you for the snacks."

There are several reports of Lilly playing ball with visitors to the Civil War section of the hospital. One of the most detailed reports comes from that same tour group. The woman who brought the ball and the candy set the ball down on the middle of the floor. Shelley said the entire tour group stepped away from the ball and then watched as it rolled to the other side of the room, bounced off the wall, and rolled back to them. What followed was a forty-five-minute game of rolling the ball back and forth with Lilly.

It would seem that we can add playful and polite to the list of adjectives that describe this spirit, but according to psychic Tammy Wilson, Lilly's story is not a happy one. She says that just upstairs from where Lilly hangs out there is the spirit of a woman. A sad woman. A mother without a child. Tammy believes this to be the spirit of Lilly's mother, looking for her long-lost daughter. Unfortunately, for whatever reason, Lilly never leaves the main floor of the hospital, and her mother never leaves her room on the upper levels. The pair may spend eternity searching for one another, but stairs and building materials always separate them. What a heartbreaking thought!

Jacob

The Weston State Hospital opened to patients in 1864, toward the end of the American Civil War. Because of the timing, many of the early patients were actually soldiers suffering from the afflictions that come with combat — everything from PTSD to physical ailments like tuberculosis. Those patients were housed in the part of the hospital that has come to be known as the Civil War section. The Civil War wing is the oldest and most paranormally active part of the hospital. Although Lilly is the best-known spiritual inhabitant of this part of the hospital, she is not the only named entity people claim to have encountered. There is also Jacob.

Little is known about Jacob's life and death, or even why he was admitted to the hospital in the first place. It is said, though, that he was a soldier in the Civil War and that the best way to attract his attention is to be a pretty girl, especially one wearing perfume. It makes sense, really. If Jacob really was a soldier in the Civil War, it's no wonder that he'd go out of his way to attract the attention of a pretty girl — especially given all the horrors he would have witnessed during his time at war, exclusively in the company of men.

According to Benjamin S. Jeffries, visitors to Jacob's part of the hospital have heard coughing, laughing, footsteps, and even whispered threats. Even those who haven't actually heard or seen anything claim to feel as though they are being watched when they walk through the Civil War area.

Crouching Doctor

The Atlantic Paranormal Society (or TAPS) investigated the Trans-Allegheny Lunatic Asylum. Both Grant Wilson and Jason Hawes reported feeling uncomfortable in the Civil War part of the hospital, as though they were being hunted. Several times they thought they heard sounds like coughing or movement though there was no one there. Then they turned a corner into a unused room, and both claim to have seen a full-bodied apparition of a man. The figure crouched down and then seemed to be sucked or pulled out of the room.

"I saw a person standing down there," says Grant Wilson. "Its arms came up over its head, grabbed its head, and it crouched down to the floor. And looked like, almost like, it got sucked back out of the room backwards."

Jason Hawes agreed with his friend's description, claiming he also saw "a man in a medical-type robe and it appeared that he just crouched down really fast, covering himself, and then jetted out of the doorway."

Neither man offered any explanation for who or what they saw, or how or why it was propelled out of the room backward. Their purported sighting, however, has an interesting parallel with something that happened to one of the facility's tour guides.

Caroline Daniels was standing just outside of one of the rooms while conducting a tour through the Civil War section. Suddenly, something jerked on her skirt and, in full view of her entire tour group, she was pulled down to the ground. She says whatever the unseen force was, it was fighting with her. "I was being captured," she reported.

Witnesses saw her slide backward, into the room. One witness claimed, "I literally had to sit on top of her to hold her still." Finally, whatever was holding her let her go, and they were able to stand up and run away.

Could this have a connection to the story Jason and Grant told about seeing a being crouch down and get pulled out of the room?

The Fourth Floor

The Civil War section might be the setting for most of the creepy stories around the Trans-Allegheny Lunatic Asylum, but it's not the only area reputed for its paranormal activity. The fourth floor is also said to be haunted, as is the way up to it.

Once when tour guide Caroline Daniels was stopped on the third-floor landing to give a little talk, she watched one member of her group wander away. Daniels continued to talk about the history of the building and waited for him to come back. When he didn't return, she asked the rest of her group to wait while she retrieved him but discovered that no one was missing. Not only was her entire group present and accounted for, she was the only person to have seen the man who'd disappeared.

The fourth floor is said to be haunted by a nurse who was murdered by a patient. Her body was concealed in an unused stairwell for weeks before she was discovered. Is it any wonder her spirit remains? It's also purportedly the home to many unnamed spirits whose footsteps, crying, screaming, and moaning have all been reported by visitors.

Sue Parker, a retired psychiatric aide who worked at the Weston State Hospital for thirty years, says she knew the fourth floor was haunted because when she'd go up there she could hear someone, or something, following her. One day she finally said, "Why are you following me? I don't want to hurt you. Show me what you want." The response? A heavy hospital door slammed. "That sure got my attention," she says.

And perhaps that really is all they wanted — a little bit of attention. The owner of Trans-Allegheny Lunatic Asylum, Rebecca Jordan, says many visitors report hearing the sound of children running up and down the fourth floor hallways, playing and giggling. I think we all know how far some children will go to get our attention.

It's important to remember that, as with many closed hospitals, the Trans-Allegheny Lunatic Asylum is currently owned by private individuals who use funds raised from historical tours and ghost hunts to pay for the facility's restoration and maintenance. Thus, the better the stories coming out of its walls, the better it is for them. Are some of the reports of paranormal activity overhyped then? Perhaps it is so, but overhyped or not, these are still good stories.

REST OF THE WORLD

ITALY

Palermo Hospital: The Disturbed Inmates

Palermo, Rome
The following is an exact copy of an archived newspaper article that appeared in the *Altoona Mirror* on March 18, 1927.

> THE HAUNTED HOSPITAL. Rome. March 18. The inmates of a hospital at Palermo have been much disturbed by the supposed visit of "spirits," which were accused by two night nurses of pulling their hair. On one occasion the wards echoed with eerie cries of a nurse haunted, as she declared, by pursuing ghosts, and it took all the persuasion of the chaplain and much sprinkling of holy water before the patients could be persuaded to return to their beds. There had been a stampede down the wards. Upon the nurses being given a room that they approve of, the "spirits" have been laid to rest without a miracle.

Poveglia Island: Real Life "Shutter Island"

Venice

Welcome to the place some people call the real life "Shutter Island." If the legends are to be believed, Poveglia Island is composed of one part human remains and one part earth.

From the air Poveglia Island, located in the Venetian Lagoon, looks like a lush green paradise, but its shadowy history is filled with so many unimaginable horrors that it is surrounded as much by rumours and superstition as it is the Mediterranean Sea.

Panorama of Poveglia Island (Venice) as seen from the Lido.

Plague Island

In the 1770s Poveglia Island began functioning under the jurisdiction of the *Magistrato alla Sanità*, or the public health office, as a sort of checkpoint for ships bringing cargo into Venice. In 1793 several cases of plague were found on two ships coming through this checkpoint. As a result, the island became a quarantine zone for those afflicted with the plague, but this is only the most recent example of Poveglia being a plague island — sadly, it played this role over and over again in its long and bloody history.

In the days of antiquity, the Romans used the isolated little island as a quarantine zone, leaving their diseased people there to die. Later, when plague again threatened the known world, Venetians picked up where the Romans left off and Poveglia Island became one of three quarantine islands, or lazarettos, in the Venetian Lagoon.

The situation was often much more humane than one might imagine. American writer and filmmaker Ransom Riggs, who visited Poveglia Island in 2010, reported that at Lazaretto Poveglia, "Most wayfarers had their own room, sometimes even their own little apartment. They were fed well and drank together and they could send and receive mail."

However, Venice underwent many full-blown plague outbreaks, and during those periods "there's little doubt that the lazarettos turned from Purgatory into Hell."

Venice had very strict sanitation laws, and those who were sick, or even just suspected of being sick, were rounded up and taken to the island, left there to live or die as they might. In fact, the stories say that the ferries carrying the sick and the dead to the island for isolation or disposal ran continuously at peak points of the plague. To achieve the latter, large numbers of corpses, the bodies of plague victims, were stacked in plague pits on the north side of the island and burned. That putrid smoke would have filled the air over the island and been visible for miles and miles — bringing fear and dread to the hearts of everyone who witnessed it.

Worse even than the horror of the plague pits on the north end of the island, or the stories of body parts tumbling into the sea, are the stories of people being thrown into the infernos while still alive. It is said that during the peak outbreaks of plague, people who were unwell but still alive were accidentally thrown into the flaming pits as panicked workers struggled to send every carrier of the plague — human or otherwise — up in smoke as quickly as possible. Sadly, there are also stories of premeditation.

The eastern side of the island has a large open area known as the Plague Fields, so called because it is where large numbers of plague sufferers abided, waiting for the disease to claim them. That seems horrifying enough, but there are also stories about doctors and guards who would patrol these fields and take those near death to the Burning Grounds to be fed to the flames. There were no peaceful deaths for those afflicted with the Black Death. If the plague didn't get you, the fires would.

The screams of the burning carried almost all the way across the lagoon to Venice. How must it have felt to approach the island on a ferry and hear those agonized wails coming across the water, growing louder and louder as you drew closer to your own destination? How terrifying to hear your painful future fate and not be able to avoid it.

It is said that even now these tormented souls linger. Misty apparitions have been spotted moving over the Plague Fields, and voices have been heard by visitors and captured on EVP. Nearer to the burning grounds, screams and wails have been heard and the phantom odours of burning flesh and hair have been reported.

Estimates of the number of people cremated or buried on Poveglia Island over its entire history vary widely, but many accounts pin the number at 160,000 or more. That is an awful lot of human remains on a seventeen-acre island. This explains why urban legends claim half of the island is made up of human remains and describe a thick layer of oily ash that covers the island's surface. In fact, many stories say there are so many dead that the island can't contain them all; even today fishermen who cast their nets too close to Poveglia Island occasionally discover human bones alongside the fish in their nets. Though these bones have no doubt entered the ocean through natural means, such as erosion, it is no less unnerving to think that there are so many bodies there that the land can no longer hold them all, spilling them into the sea.

If the stories are to be believed, plague wasn't the only reason for being burned alive on Poveglia Island. Starting in 1645 a series of octagonal-shaped fortified islands were created in the Venetian Lagoon, meant to repel Genoese invaders. One of the islands was separated from Poveglia Island by only a narrow channel. In addition to whatever killings can be ascribed to the area in its capacity against invaders, it was also used by the English to ambush French commandos during the Napoleonic Wars. Legend says that prisoners who were caught this way were taken to Poveglia Island and burned, just as the plague victims once had been. The same stories also say that numerous sunken French ships recline in the seabed surrounding the octagon, adding to the number of dead and the degree of suffering that can be associated with the island.

Insane Asylum

In 1922 the island and its buildings were repurposed once more. Part of the island was used as a mental hospital while another part may have been used as a retirement community. One of the most frequently told and eerie stories about Poveglia Island takes place during this time. It is said that one of the doctors working at the mental hospital, Dr. Damyan Nikolovich, noticed a disproportionately high number of his patients were suffering from phasmophobia, essentially a paralyzing fear of ghosts, coupled with phantasmagoria — the delusion of seeing ghosts.

Patient after patient told the doctor disconcertingly similar stories of seeing terrifying spirits — the ghosts of plague victims, smelling the odour of burning bodies, and hearing threatening whispers when they were alone. Being a man of science, Dr. Nikolovich dismissed their claims as a shared delusion brought on by the ghost stories around Poveglia Island's dark history. This would come back to haunt him — pun intended — later.

Driven to leave his name in the annals of psychiatric discovery, the doctor began using experimental treatments of his own devising on his patients. He is alleged to have performed lobotomies — perforating patients' brains in order to shut down the parts of them suspected of causing their insanity — with tools as primitive as drills, hammers, and chisels. Then, perhaps influenced by the same dark forces his patients complained of, he went even further.

We were unable to discover any specific allegations against the doctor, but the legend says experimental surgeries and treatments that "bordered on absolute butchery" were the norm for those under Dr. Nikolovich's care. Further, many of these torturous surgeries and experiments are said to have taken place in the bell tower.

After years of torturing his patients in the name of science, the doctor went mad. He climbed to the top of the bell tower and jumped to his death.

Some stories say his patients revolted, carried him to the top of the tower, and threw him off, but the only way to the top of the bell tower is by way of a 150-foot ladder. That would be difficult enough for one person to climb, let alone several unwell people carrying a full-grown man who didn't want to be carried. Others have suggested he was driven mad by the very same ghosts and dark forces that tormented his patients (and which he had thought to be only shared delusions). Or perhaps, more mundanely, he was driven to suicide by the guilt over the torturous experiments he'd put his patients through.

Our favourite story, however, is the one that says after decades of performing heinous procedures on his patients, the doctor began to see the plague-ridden spirits that inhabit Poveglia Island for himself. Forced to admit they were real and not just the delusions of his patients, he was led to the tower by his guilt, or by the spirits themselves. In this story, when the doctor jumped from the tower, the fall did not immediately kill him. No. He lay on the ground, his wrecked body seizing and shuddering in pain while a nurse rushed to help. She stopped in her tracks, however, when she saw a mist come up out of the ground and choke the doctor to death.

The hospital was closed in 1968 and the island shut down to tourism. Even today it is difficult to find someone who will take you there, and those who do are rarely willing to set foot on the property. People who do investigate it, however, find it a paradoxical place that is filled with natural beauty and suffused with a sense of peace while still bearing the marks of its grotesque and disturbing history.

Photographer Mike Deere recently visited Poveglia Island and said, "the overwhelming feeling I experienced during my time there was actually one of peace and serenity — it was a very quiet place." And yet, he added, "I'm not going to forget the soil composition of the burning grounds in a hurry."

In 2014 the cash-strapped Italian government decided to auction off a ninety-nine-year lease of Poveglia Island. A businessman, Luigi Brugnaro, won that auction for £400,000. His intentions are to restore some of the island's derelict buildings and open it up for public use once again. Though there's no information available as to what form that will take — a luxury hotel, perhaps? A tourist attraction? — one can only imagine that once people are more easily able to visit Poveglia Island, its fame will grow and the stories around it will multiply. Will it become a peaceful retreat, the most haunted place on earth, or both? Only time will tell.

SINGAPORE

Old Changi Hospital:
Malaysian Vampires and Blood-Soaked Beaches

Changi
Malaysian and Indonesian folklore contains a creature called a pontianak, which is like a female vampiric ghost. Pontianaks are generally portrayed

as pale-skinned women with long black hair and red eyes, wearing blood-spattered white dresses. They are said to be the spirits of women who died while they were pregnant, and they haunt the night looking for men to prey upon. Once they choose a victim, Pontianaks transform into beautiful seductresses — beautiful until they dig their talon-like fingernails into your stomach to devour your organs. Pontianaks can be identified by the strong floral fragrance that surrounds them (remember this, it's going to be important) before morphing into the stench of rotting flesh, and they are just one category of the unearthly things that have been spotted roaming the grounds and surrounding countryside of the Old Changi Hospital.

A Little History

In 1935 Singapore was still a British colony. That year the Crown built the Old Changi Hospital up on a hill in Changi, Singapore, as both a barracks and hospital. When it first opened, it was called the Royal Air Force Hospital and served largely as a military facility. When the Second World War broke out, the Japanese invaded and took over the hospital and barracks, using them as a prison camp run by their secret police, the Kempeitai.

The Kempeitai are notorious for having used fear and torture to get information and to punish those who crossed them. They enthusiastically employed every kind of torture you can imagine, and many you won't want to. From rape to biological warfare, it would seem nothing was too extreme. Some of their atrocities seem like things straight out of a movie — throwing caged prisoners into the ocean to drown or be eaten alive by sharks, or, worse, cutting limbs off people and then sewing them back on in different locations to see what happened. While it's impossible to say for certain exactly what the Kempeitai did within the walls of the hospital during the war, it is safe to assume that it was the stuff of nightmares.

When the war was drawing to a close, the tables turned on the Japanese occupiers. Once Singapore was liberated from Japanese military control, Japanese soldiers were the ones who faced execution — often in the same place they had committed horrible acts against the friends and families of those who were now their captors.

Eventually the hospital and barracks were all converted back into a hospital. It operated in its hillside location until the 1990s, when it was relocated to make access easier for patients and staff, who would no longer have to deal with the steep staircases throughout the grounds. The buildings that had seen so much trauma and abuse were left to stand empty but for the spirits that haunt them.

Changi Hauntings

Starting as far back as the 1940s, when the hospital was in operation after the war, people began reporting paranormal experiences in and around Old Changi Hospital: things like disembodied screams that sound as though they've been ripped from the lungs of a person in the throes of horrific torture, full apparitions, shadow people, and erratic lights. One common sighting is that of a small boy sitting all by himself and staring into space. Other frequently reported ghosts include a baby crawling through the empty hallways of the abandoned hospital and a white-haired Chinese lady in a broken-down wheelchair.

Further, according to the website Unexplained Mysteries of the World, villagers talk of seeing the spirits of people of several different nationalities wandering around the hospital grounds and even through the village itself. There are stories of ghostly Japanese soldiers wearing the fear-inducing uniforms of the Imperial Guard from the Second World War, and the spirits of Chinese soldiers who were tortured and killed in the hospital during its occupation have been spotted, as well. Even Caucasian ghosts belonging to British soldiers make appearances now and then. The prevailing theory is that these are the ghosts of soldiers from both sides of the conflict who perished in the area.

And, according to *Lost in the Darkness* by Benjamin S. Jeffries, the ghosts don't limit themselves to the hospital grounds and village either. The beaches surrounding Old Changi were the scene for mass carnage; Chinese citizens and sympathizers who didn't swear allegiance to Japan were beheaded there. Some stories say the number of dead were in the hundreds of thousands, but even if we assume that's an exaggeration, it seems safe to say the beaches would have run red with blood. Nowadays, so the story says, ghostly decapitated bodies occasionally wash up on the beach, and occasionally a spectral head will be spotted soaring through the air as if it had just been relieved of its body.

Led Astray

One of the creepiest occurrences at Old Changi Hospital is also, apparently, one of its most common.

As the stories and rumours about Old Changi Hospital expand, so does its appeal to a certain segment of society — those who like to brush up against the unknown. These people will venture into Old Changi Hospital, looking to encounter the unexplainable or simply to enjoy a good scare. Sometimes they get a little bit more than they bargained for.

The stories, in particular those reported on the Paranormal Guide website (dedicated to "all things paranormal, strange, dark and macabre"), say that while exploring the empty, echoing halls of Old Changi Hospital, one member of the group will be persuaded by another to separate from the rest of the group. The pair of friends will then venture off on their own, going deeper and deeper into the hospital. Everything will seem normal — conversation, behaviour — right up until the friend who talked them into leaving the main group disappears.

Suddenly, the explorer realizes that he is lost in the dark, alone but for whatever spirits still linger there, in one of the most haunted places in Singapore. Once the wanderer is eventually found, terrified and disoriented, he learns from his group of friends that he had wandered off alone, not with a friend as he believed. Certainly without any *human* companions.

In another variation on this encounter, the explorer is led, not deeper into the hospital, but out of it by a "friend" who says that they don't belong there because it's too dangerous, and that they should not return. That friend also disappears once the paranormal explorer has been guided safely back out of the building.

The Changi Pontianak

In researching haunted hospitals to write this book we encountered a lot of common threads — female spirits named Mary, for example, and balls left in hallways for childish ghosts to play with. One thing that is absolutely unique to Old Changi Hospital, as far as we can tell, is the pontianak said to haunt the grounds and village.

Sightings of a pontianak have been reported in and around the Old Changi Hospital for years. It is said this creature appears and disappears at will. One man, a former patient of Old Changi named Ah-Toh, is said to have seen and smelled something unnerving during his time in the hospital. In his words,

> During my two weeks stay, I saw occasional shadows moving about on the ceilings of the corridor when it's empty, and heard some coughing near me, even though I'm the only patient in the ward, during days and nights. There was once I woke up to a strong flower perfume on a particularly cold night. Tried everything: increase the speed of the ceiling fan, rub tiger balm near the nose. The perfume disappeared when a nurse came in during a routine check.

Remember the thing at the beginning of this chapter about the smell that accompanied the appearance of a pontianak? If that was the cause of the smell Ah-Toh experienced, perhaps it was better that he never spotted it.

THE UNITED KINGDOM

Severalls Hospital: Bombed by the Nazis

Colchester, England

The Second Essex County Asylum opened in 1913 in order to alleviate some of the overcrowding at the (first) Essex County Asylum. The first hospital eventually came to be called Warley Hospital, and the second, Severalls Hospital, or Severalls Mental Hospital.

The wards at Severalls were originally segregated by gender — even staff weren't allowed to enter the opposite gender's ward. Those rules were soon relaxed, but there were still men's and women's sides.

When the First World War broke out, the hospital was commandeered and turned into a military facility. Originally it served as a military camp and then, as the war became worse and there were more wounded soldiers to deal with, as a military hospital. When the war ended, the hospital was decommissioned and returned to civilian use.

Tragically, in the very early hours of the morning of August 11, 1942, in the midst of the Second World War, the Luftwaffe (German air force) dropped three five-hundred-pound bombs on the hospital. They landed on the women's ward, killing thirty-eight women and injuring twenty-three more. Dozens of stories of heroism and selflessness are told about that night as people laboured for hours to save those trapped in the debris.

After a long, colourful history, Severalls Hospital closed its doors in 1997, and a "ring of steel" was erected around the site to try to keep trespassers out. It proved less than effective, and the hospital suffered at least two arson attacks in the years that followed. The site abounds with illegally visiting ghost hunters.

There are few, if any, detailed descriptions of paranormal experiences at Severalls Hospital, but the *Urban Ghost* crew captured some interesting evidence of activity on the grounds. In one hallway they took a photograph of a hazy outline that looks like it could be a human figure, which they suggest might be the spirit of a nurse pushing an invisible wheelchair. They also have a photograph of some orbs hovering in a room containing an empty hospital bed and what looks like a few propane tanks. Just outside that room they've captured an EVP of a man's voice saying, "I live."

Royal Hospital: Asking for Help from a Ghostly Roman Soldier

Derby, England

Shortly after the Royal Hospital opened its doors, reports of a ghost began to pour in. People reported seeing a man dressed all in black with a cloak. Apparently the man could walk through walls. Since the hospital site used to be an ancient Roman road, people tend to think the spirit is the ghost of a Roman soldier who died there.

A 2009 *Daily Mail* article reported that hospital administrators were taking the sightings seriously — so seriously, in fact, that they actually hired an exorcist to rid the property of the ghost in order to put the staff's minds to rest. But at least one staff member was a fan of the ghost. Said the anonymous cleaner, "I'd quite like to see a ghost. Perhaps it could help out when we're understaffed."

RAF Hospital Nocton Hall: Upstaged by a Tree

Nocton, Lincolnshire, England

Nocton Hall is unique among the hospitals that we investigated because it is actually more famous for a tree growing on its grounds than it is for being haunted. Nocton Hall began its life as a private home. Built in 1530, this estate has housed several famous residents, including Frederick John Robinson, 1st Earl of Ripon, who, for a short time, was the Prime Minster of the United Kingdom.

During both the First and Second World Wars the hospital was commandeered and used first as a convalescent home and then as a hospital. It returned to service as a private residence in the 1980s but was leased back to the army for use during the Gulf War in 1984. In 1994 it officially closed its doors. Sadly, it was badly burned in 2004 and now stands only in ruins.

Though stories circulate about the grounds of Nocton Hall being haunted by the ghosts of the men and women who worked and died there, very few patients actually passed through the doorway of this hospital. This, coupled with the fact that it's difficult to find specific stories about hauntings, makes most of the ghost stories surrounding Nocton Hall feel a bit like general atmosphere — most, not all.

One story seems to be repeated over and over — that of the ghost of a traumatized young woman. In a *Grantham Journal* article, she is said to haunt one particular bedroom more than the rest. This girl is said to have woken several visitors at exactly 4:30 a.m. The startled visitors wake to find the ghostly girl at the foot of their bed, sobbing and mumbling about a devilish man. Some people even claim to have captured an image of the girl on film. The story goes on to allege that this ghost is the spirit of a girl who was raped and murdered on the grounds, but we weren't able to find any official records to confirm whether that ever happened.

Even more famous at Nocton Hall than the sobbing ghost, however, is a tree that grows just outside it. It must be tough for a ghost to be upstaged by a tree, but if it's going to happen, this is the tree you want to do it. It is a massive chestnut tree that stands with the help of some reinforcing boards. It is reported that the now-giant tree was planted in 1541 by Catherine Howard — the fifth wife of King Henry VIII.

Newsham Park Hospital:
A Ghost Child's Image Caught on Film

Liverpool, England

According to the Haunted Places website, before it was converted into a hospital, the now-abandoned Newsham Park Hospital building used to be an orphanage. Many investigators claim to have picked up the presence of a child's spirit there. The building is also said to have an oppressive atmosphere, and the sound of running and dragging feet can be heard echoing through the dark.

A February 2015 article in the *Daily Mirror* reported a much talked-about eerie sight — not something recorded by a paranormal investigator, but rather an image captured on a geographical mapping service run by one of the world's largest tech companies.

A Google Street View image captured what appears to be a face in the window of the old deserted building. A local resident spotted the image on the open-access mapping tool, which is built into Google Maps and Google Earth, and shared his find. The face is believed to be that of a mysterious ghost child.

St. Thomas's Hospital: Ghostly Doctor Caught on Camera

Stockport, England

St. Thomas's Hospital had been sitting vacant and in disrepair for almost a dozen years when Jamie-Leigh Brown went exploring in the spring of 2015. A *Daily Mail* article reported that the woman was startled to learn that a photo she took at St. Thomas's appears to show the ghostly image of a doctor.

That's just one of the creepy tales surrounding this building, which started out as a union workhouse on Christmas Day in 1841. Later it was renamed Shaw Health Hospital in the 1940s and finally, in 1954, it became known as St. Thomas's Hospital until it closed its doors in 2004.

The institution, home to an unprecedented number of poor, homeless, and unemployed during the nineteenth century, was also known by the nickname the "Grubber." In 1895 inmates of the dangerously overcrowded workhouse were said to have been "packed in like sardines," with far more than the 690 residents the housing was intended for. Conditions became deplorable and unruly, resulting in a violent riot.

Often considered one of the most terrifying and disturbing locations by ghost investigators, St. Thomas's Hospital was the subject of a full episode of the British television series *Most Haunted*. On the program, host Yvette Fielding and a team of parapsychologists, mediums, and other staff would lock themselves into a haunted location overnight in order to investigate and explore the science, psychology, and evidence associated with various hauntings.

In *Most Haunted*'s ninth season, on the episode that aired February 13, 2007, Fielding introduced the location, describing how the building was said to be alive with a significant amount of spiritual activity and a general feeling of overall uneasiness. She reported that EMF meters in the building displayed wild fluctuations.

There had been numerous reports of ghostly apparitions appearing throughout the building, low moans heard in the dead of night, and muffled sounds of screaming coming from both the women's wing and the lunatic asylum. They also mentioned that, before the building had been closed in 2004, the top floor was so haunted that staff were no longer allowed there.

One of the spirits who made herself known was a dominant feminine presence in the women's wing. She seemed to get extremely agitated by the presence of any men in that area. When walking through the master's quarters in the Stockport workhouse episode, medium David Wells spoke about the spirit of a woman named Annie, whose presence was felt. He reported that she was whispering messages into his ear, most notably, "Prepare yourself for the horrors ahead."

During the overnight filming, one investigator, Cath, seemed to have been affected by a spirit during an ad hoc seance. She began to feel a strange choking feeling in her throat, finding it difficult to breath and launching into a coughing fit. Shortly after the seance, as the crew were leaving the kitchen area, they were startled by the unexpected sound of glass shattering behind them. When they trained their lights and cameras on the source of the sound, they found the glass they had used on the tabletop for their seance had been flung against a radiator, where it smashed.

Throughout the episode odd knocks and loud violent thumping sounds can be heard. Watching the program, complete with its eerie music and startling video effects, leaves the viewer with chills and a sense of constant fearfulness.

Most Haunted has not been without controversy, however, with multiple reports of leaked video footage and claims by former staff members that the hosts had faked many of the thrown objects and knocks in the dark. In May 2013 an in-depth article by Matt Roper in the *Mirror* provided information from Dr. Ciaran O'Keefe, a parapsychologist whose skeptical presence on the show was meant to give it an element of credibility. After viewer complaints, Ofcom, an independent broadcasting regulator in the UK, stated that in the show "techniques are used which mean the audience is not necessarily in full possession of the facts." Ofcom ultimately ruled that the antics were not fraud because *Most*

Haunted was touted as an entertainment program rather than a legitimate investigation into the paranormal.

A few years after the *Most Haunted* controversy, a twenty-one-year-old woman and her friends captured a chilling image in a photograph while exploring inside the building. When Jamie-Leigh Brown and her friends entered St. Thomas's to look around and have a bit of a laugh, they kept hearing odd footsteps and shuffling noises coming from the floor above them in the abandoned building. After only a few minutes inside the building, they became spooked and fled. It was only after they left that she examined one of the photographs she had taken inside. In the distance behind one of her friends, the image of a doctor can be seen standing in an elevator shaft.

"It freaked me out," Jamie-Leigh told the *London Sun* in a May 2015 article. "It's really creepy to think my friend was just heading towards the area where the ghost was."

Other figures, such as a radiant woman dressed as either a nurse or a nun have been seen in the building, according to listings on the Paranormal Database website.

If the building is truly haunted by former patients — or even residents whose conditions made them feel more like inmates — one wonders what might be in store for the building and grounds when Stockport College, who acquired the site, refurbishes it as part of their campus expansion.

Unidentified Garrison Hospital: Ghost Writing

Location Undisclosed, England

During our research we found an intriguing tale contained within one of the very first studies of the supernatural to come from the English speaking world. Catherine Crowe (1803–76) was an English novelist and children's writer. Her 1848 book *The Night Side of Nature: Or, Ghosts and Ghost Seers* went on to become her most popular work, being translated into multiple languages, including French and German.

The book is a series of sketches and anecdotes that Crowe gathered, not for amusement, but rather to emphasize the supernatural and to encourage readers to keep an open mind about incidents reported throughout history by all cultures. As she wrote, "we should avail ourselves of the instruction to be gained by the simple knowledge that such phenomena have existed and been observed in all ages; and that thereby our connection with the spiritual world may become a demonstrated fact to all who choose to open their eyes to it."

The following is an excerpt that shares the tale of a soldier laid up in a hospital ward who is visited by the ghost of a woman whose burial he had been involved in just one year earlier. The woman instructs him to write down a secret to be shared with her husband, who is still alive. The soldier is then made to keep the details of what she has communicated to her husband a secret from anyone else.

> In narrating the following story, I am not permitted to give the names of the place or parties, nor the number of the regiment, with all of which however I am acquainted. The account was taken down by one of the officers, with whose family I am also acquainted; and the circumstance occurred within the last ten years.
>
> "About the month of August," says Captain E., "my attention was requested by the school-master-sergeant, a man of considerable worth, and highly esteemed by the whole corps, to an event which had occurred in the garrison hospital. Having heard his recital, which, from the serious earnestness with which he made it, challenged attention, I resolved to investigate the matter; and having communicated the circumstances to a friend, we both repaired to the hospital for the purpose of enquiry.
>
> "There were two patients to be examined — both men of good character, and neither of them suffering from any disorder affecting the brain; the one was under treatment for consumptive symptoms, and the other for an ulcerated leg; and they were both in the prime of life.
>
> "Having received a confirmation of the school-master's statement from the hospital-sergeant, also a very

respectable and trustworthy man, I sent for the patient principally concerned, and desired him to state what he had seen and heard, warning him, at the same time, that it was my intention to take down his deposition, and that it behoved him to be very careful, as, possibly, serious steps might be taken for the purpose of discovering whether an imposition had been practiced in the wards of the hospital — a crime for which, he was well aware, a very severe penalty would be inflicted. He then proceeded to relate the circumstances, which I took down in the presence of Mr. B., and the hospital-sergeant, as follows:

"'It was last Tuesday night, somewhere between eleven and twelve, when all of us were in bed, and all lights out except the rush-light that was allowed for the man with the fever, when I was awoke by feeling a weight upon my feet, and at the same moment, as I was drawing up my pegs, Private W., who lies in the cot opposite mine, called out, "I say, Q. there's somebody sitting upon your legs!" and as I looked to the bottom of my bed, I saw some one get up from it, and then come round and stand over me, in the passage betwixt my cot and the next. I felt somewhat alarmed; for the last few nights the ward had been disturbed by sounds as of a heavy foot walking up and down; and as nobody could be seen, it was beginning to be supposed amongst us that it was haunted, and fancying this that came up to my bed's head might be the ghost, I called out, "Who are you and what do you want?"

"'The figure then leaning, with one hand on the wall, over my head, and stooping down, said, in my ear, "I am Mrs. M.;" and I could then distinguish that she was dressed in a flannel gown, edged with black ribbon, exactly similar to a set of grave clothes in which I had assisted to clothe her corpse, when her death took place a year previously.

"'The voice however was not like Mrs. M.'s, nor like anybody else's, yet it was very distinct, and seemed somehow to sing through my head. I could see nothing of a face beyond a darkish colour about the head, and it appeared to me that I could see through her body against the window-glasses.

"'Although I felt very uncomfortable, I asked her what she wanted. She replied, "I am Mrs. M., and I wish you to write to him that was my husband, and tell him...."'

"'I am not, sir,' said Corporal Q., 'at liberty to mention to anybody what she told me, except to her husband. He is at the depot in Ireland, and I have written and told him. She made me promise not to tell any one else. After I had promised secrecy, she told me something of a matter, that convinced me I was talking to a spirit; for it related to what only I and Mrs. M. knew, and no one living could know anything whatever of the matter; and if I was not speaking my last words on earth, I say solemnly that it was Mrs. M.'s spirit that spoke to me then, and no one else. After promising that if I complied with her request, she would not trouble me or the ward again, she went from my bed towards the fireplace, and with her hands she kept feeling about the wall over the mantel-piece. After awhile, she came towards me again; and whilst my eyes were upon her, she somehow disappeared from my sight altogether, and I was left alone.

"'It was then that I felt faint like, and a cold sweat broke out over me; but I did not faint, and after a time I got better, and gradually I went off to sleep.

"'The men in the ward said, next day, that Mrs. M. had come to speak to me about purgatory, because she had been a Roman Catholic, and we had often had arguments on religion: but what she told me had no reference to such subjects, but to a matter only she and I knew of.'

"After closely cross-questioning Corporal Q., and endeavouring, without success, to reason him out of his belief in the ghostly character of his visitor; I read over to him what I had written, and then, dismissing him, sent for the other patient.

"After cautioning him, as I had done the first, I proceeded to take down his statement, which was made with every appearance of good faith and sincerity.

"'I was lying awake,' said he, 'last Tuesday night, when I saw some one sitting on Corporal Q.'s bed. There was so little light in the ward that I could not make out who it was, and the figure looked so strange that I got alarmed, and felt quite sick. I called out to Corporal Q. that there was somebody sitting upon his bed, and then the figure got up; and as I did not know but it might be coming to me, I got so much alarmed, that being but weakly (this was the consumptive man) I fell back, and I believe I fainted away. When I got round again, I saw the figure standing, and apparently talking to the Corporal, placing one hand against the wall and stopping down. I could not however hear any voice; and being still much alarmed, I put my head under the clothes for a considerable time. When I looked up again I could only see Corporal Q., sitting up in bed alone, and he said he had seen a ghost; and I told him I had also seen it. After a time, he got up and gave me a drink of water, for I was very faint. Some of the other patients being disturbed by our talking, they bid us be quiet, and after some time I got to sleep. The ward has not been disturbed since.'

"The man was then cross-questioned; but his testimony remaining quite unshaken, he was dismissed, and the hospital-sergeant was interrogated, with regard to the possibility of a trick having been practiced. He asserted, however, that this was impossible; and, certainly, from my own knowledge of the hospital regulations, and the habits of the patients, I should say that a practical joke of this nature was too serious a thing to have been attempted by anybody, especially as there were patients in the ward, very ill at the time, and one very near his end. The punishment would have been extremely severe, and discovery almost certain, since everybody would have been adverse to the delinquent.

"The investigation that ensued was a very brief one, it being found that there was nothing more to be elicited; and the affair terminated with the supposition that the two men had been dreaming. Nevertheless, six months afterwards, on being interrogated, their evidence and their conviction were as clear as at first, and they declared themselves ready at any time to repeat their statement upon oath."

Supposing this case to be as the men believed it, there are several things worthy of observation. In the first place, the ghost is guilty of that inconsistency so offensive to Francis Grose, and many others. Instead of telling her secret to her husband, she commissions the Corporal to tell it to him, and it is not till a year after her departure from this life that she does even that; and she is heard in the ward two or three nights before she is visible. We are therefore constrained to suppose that like Mrs. Bretton, she could not communicate with her husband, and that till that Tuesday night, the necessary conditions for attaining her object, as regarded the Corporal, were wanting. It is also remarkable, that although the latter heard her speak distinctly, and spoke to her, the other man heard no voice; which renders it probable, that she had at length been able to produce that impression upon him, which a magnetiser does on his somnambule, enabling each to understand the other by a transference of thought, which was indistinguishable to the Corporeal from speaking, as it is frequently to the somnambule. The imitating the actions of life by leaning against the wall and feeling about the mantel-piece, are very unlike what a person would have done, who was endeavouring to impose on the man; and equally unlike what they would have reported, had the thing been an invention of their own.

Amongst the established jests on the subject of ghosts, their sudden vanishing, is a very fruitful one; but, I think, if we examine this question, we shall find, that there is nothing comical in the matter, except the ignorance or want of reflection of the jesters.

In the first place, as I have before observed, a spirit must be where its thoughts and affections are, for they are itself — *our* spirits are where our thoughts and affections are, although our solid bodies remain stationary; and no one will suppose, that walls or doors, or material obstacles of any kind, could exclude a spirit, any more than they can exclude our thoughts.

But then, there is the visible body of the spirit — what is that? And how does it retain its shape! For we know, that there is a law discovered by Dalton, that two masses of gaseous matter cannot remain in contact, but they will immediately proceed to diffuse themselves into one another; and accordingly, it may be advanced, that a gaseous corporeity in the atmosphere, is an impossibility, because it could not retain its form, but would inevitably be dissolved away, and blend with the surrounding air. But precisely the same objection might be made by a chemist to the possibility of our fleshy bodies retaining their integrity and compactness: for the human body, taken as a whole, is known to be an impossible chemical compound, except for the vitality which upholds it; and no sooner is life withdrawn from it than it crumbles into putrescence; and it is undeniable, that the aeriform body would be an impossible mechanical phenomenon, but for the vitality which, we are entitled to suppose, may uphold it. But, just as the state or condition of organization protects the fleshly body from the natural re-actions which would destroy it, so many an analogous condition of organization protect a spiritual ethereal body from the destructive influence of the mutual inter-diffusion of gases.

Thus, supposing this aeriform body to be a permanent appurtenance of the spirit, we see how it may subsist and retain its integrity, and it would be reasonable to hope to exclude the electric fluid by walls or doors as to exclude by them this subtle, fluent form. If, on the contrary, the shape be only one constructed out of the atmosphere, by an act of will, the same act of will, which is a vital force, will preserve it entire, till the will being withdrawn, it dissolves away. In either case, the moment the will or thought of the spirit is elsewhere, it is gone — it has vanished.

For those who prefer the other hypothesis, namely, that there is no outstanding shape at all, but that the will of the spirit, acting on the constructive imagination of the seer, enables him to conceive the form, as the spirit itself conceives of it, there can be no difficulty in understanding, that the becoming invisible will depend merely on a similar act of will.

Roe Valley Hospital: The Nurse with the Dead Baby

Limavady, Northern Ireland

An article in the *Londonderry Sentinel* from November 17, 2009, documents a photograph that shows a nurse-like figure holding a baby. In the photograph, taken by a nighttime security guard with a digital camera, the woman and child are wearing bonnets and clothing from a time suggestive of the building's early years. The guard only noticed the peculiar figures in it afterwards.

The photograph was convincing and disconcerting enough for the guard's skeptical supervisor to pass it along to a local paranormal society for further investigation.

One gruesome tale from the building's history, which makes the discovery of the picture that much more intriguing, is that of a pregnant nurse who allegedly kept her pregnancy a secret. She finally delivered the baby, all on her own, then killed it out of desperation. Shortly thereafter, consumed by remorse and guilt, she took her own life by hanging.

Darren Ansell, Chairman of the Paranormal Society of Ireland (formerly known as the Northern Ireland Paranormal Society), also shared the fact that during his investigations of the building, the unexplained sound of knocking and the eerie disembodied sound of a baby crying could be heard.

Ravenspark Asylum: Long-Buried Secrets

Irvine, Scotland

Ravenspark Asylum closed in 1996 and remained empty until the building was sold to real estate developers in the early 2000s for development into luxury condominiums. Most of its buildings have now been demolished, but the legacy of this building, its history, and its horrific secrets continue to make themselves felt.

Originally the Cunninghame Combination Poorhouse, it was built between 1857 and 1858. According to the website the Workhouse, it comprised a number of different local parishes, with expansion that included accommodation for the governor, a chapel, cobbles, a bakehouse, a bathhouse, and a poorhouse accommodation for ten male and ten female "pauper imbeciles and idiots."

A report from the general superintendent of poorhouses in the year 1892 claimed that paupers who died there were buried in an enclosed part of the garden if their bodies were not claimed by friends. Those records seem to be lost in the sands of time, however, and the facts only resurfaced at a much later date.

Military forces took control of the location during the First World War, and in 1930 local authorities assumed responsibility, cared for the elderly and the insane, and renamed the location Cunninghame Home and Hospital. In 1948 the new National Health Service took over, and ten years later the facility was renamed yet again, becoming Ravenspark Hospital, where both geriatric and psychiatric care were administered.

The Ghost Hunters of Scotland, a team of paranormal investigators, had long cited Ravenspark as a favourite due to the extremely active paranormal incidents recorded there. On multiple occasions, Debra Campbell and Alex Dorrens, members of Ghost Hunters of Scotland, recorded the sounds of phantom footsteps, whispered voices, and slamming doors. Their electrical equipment, though fully charged, was instantly drained of all power when brought onto the site, and EMF readings were consistently erratic.

A spirit who identified himself to investigators as "Peek-a-boo Pete" often followed the team as they traversed down the dark corridors of the building. Campbell and Dorrens learned through their research that this spirit was not of a child, but a man by the name of Peter Brown, whose mind had been stunted to the level of a child's.

However, the team did identify the spirit of an actual boy in the old physiotherapy room of the hospital. Mostly silent, this forlorn spirit of a young boy named Iain exuded an aura of angst, trapped for eternity in his tiny wheelchair.

Ward 3 is haunted by an extremely ill woman, known to impose symptoms of her illness upon those who are able to sense her. Another spirit of an aggressive orderly sends a clear message to those same sensitive visitors: he does not tolerate unwelcome guests. Campbell and Dorrens believe this angry spirit was responsible for an incident in which the door of the Annick Ward closed, preventing the team from continuing their investigation.

In December 2003, the site was slated for redevelopment by Dundas Estates, with plans to demolish most of the original structures and develop as many as seventy-five homes. That work was immediately halted, however, when workers on the site unearthed a large number of bones and human skulls. Dundas Estates issued the following statement in December 2012:

Whilst working on the Fairways View development yesterday, contractors found human remains adjacent to the historic graveyard. Police were immediately informed and construction work within the vicinity has been suspended whilst the police and forensic archaeologists deal with the remains in an appropriate and sensitive manner.

The remains of more than a dozen people were identified, and in July 2013 legal actions were made by the property owners to reinter the remains in a respectful manner. The following fall a memorial headstone was created within a special garden that commemorates the paupers who lie in still-unmarked graves. Dundas Estates redesigned its development plans to define a proper boundary for the extended graveyard.

Dundas Estates has an elaborate and beautiful website about the development, outlining its proximity to two beautiful golf clubs, the beach, schools, and leisure facilities, but there is no mention of the memorial, the graveyard, or the fact that this was the site of a poorhouse and insane asylum.

Perhaps it's just us, but there's something a little too eerie for our liking. It's too much like the premise from the 1982 film *Poltergeist* — a new housing development is built on top of an improperly relocated cemetery. Maybe we're just a little too cautious about these things. But it does lead us to wonder if perhaps, one day, the new property owners, ill-informed about the location they've chosen, might be surprised to encounter some of the restless spirits who never left the site.

THE SLEEPWALKING DEAD: A CAUTIONARY TALE

Hospital Staff (Worldwide)

This chapter isn't about any particular haunted hospital location, but instead about what has become an increasingly serious condition in general society. It's something that affects our lives and causes us to pose a danger to ourselves and others. The condition is sleep deprivation, and while it is rampant throughout society, it's most prominently felt by shift workers, including doctors and nurses.

While sleep deprivation has a negative cumulative effect on a person's physical and mental health, the condition, which presents as similar to intoxication, can seriously affect one's judgment and poses a significant danger to ourselves and to others.

In Stanley Coren's 1996 book *Sleep Thieves: An Eye-Opening Exploration into the Science and Mysteries of Sleep*, the author shows how various disasters can be traced back to sleep deprivation. He cites such incidents as the Exxon Valdez oil spill, the nuclear accidents at Three Mile Island and Chernobyl, and the space shuttle *Challenger* tragedy.

Coren walks through various aspects of sleep deprivation, revealing startling side effects. One such case describes a New York radio disc jockey named Jack Tripp who, as part of a fundraising marathon, stayed awake continuously for just over two hundred hours. Tripp displayed signs of irritability, irrationality, and the inability to think straight. He became unable to follow simple conversations and had bizarre hallucinations, including seeing bugs and spiders everywhere in his DJ booth, seeing a face staring at him from the wall clock, and believing that objects around him were changing size. Near the end of the marathon when a doctor examined him, Tripp was convinced the man was an undertaker about to bury him alive.

The Nightmare *by Henry Fuseli (1741–1825).*

Simply, the difference between the nightmare realm and reality were no longer distinguishable to Tripp. While not all sleep deprivation is as extreme, the degrees of intoxication can still have negative effects on a person's behaviour, judgment, and performance.

In a startling chapter entitled "Asleep at the Operating Table," Coren documents the malaise and how it affects professionals whose purpose it is to save lives at the most critical moments.

A *Huffington Post* article from 2014 shows that more than fifteen million Americans work irregular shifts, such as shift work, which can cause a number of health issues due to the side effects of reduced sleep. This often has a direct effect on workplace safety. The National Sleep Foundation uses the term "shift-work disorder" to describe the specific type of sleep debt incurred by shift workers, particularly overnight shift workers. This disorder also has a detrimental effect on concentration and reaction times.

Coren's chapter on hospital staff sleep deprivation opens with a story about himself. He recalls lying on a gurney in a hospital emergency room when an older nurse and a young doctor approached him. The doctor seemed to shuffle toward Coren in a listless fashion. Then he took the clipboard that contained Coren's health records and stared at it blankly for a few moments, seeming unable to focus on it. Next he asked the nurse to read it to him.

"End of shift?" the nurse asked him with a smile.

He replied in the affirmative and Coren learned that this resident was completing a twenty-four-hour shift. The nurse noted that he had what nursing staff call "end-of-shift eyes." She also mentioned that the really good doctors not only ask the nurses to read charts for them, but also request that they double-check medications and doses due to the likeliness of error.

Coren reflected that emergency rooms were likely filled with medical professionals making life-and-death decisions while suffering from massive sleep deficits. He shared a few documented cases about patients whose deaths were directly linked to the sleep debt accrued by hospital staff, including a Colorado anaesthesiologist who was charged with manslaughter after falling asleep during a routine ear operation on an eight-year-old patient. During that court case, it was revealed that the doctor had apparently fallen asleep more than half a dozen times in the previous two and a half years.

A 2012 article published on the Fierce Healthcare website opened with this question: "Is your hospital a hotspot for the walking dead?" The article went on to cite a study published in the *Archives of Surgery* that revealed further evidence that sleepy surgeons pose a significant threat to patient safety.

A study at Boston's Massachusetts General Hospital showed that surgical residents manage to get about 5.3 hours of sleep a day, with some only getting just under 3 hours. The side effect of the fatigue, the article goes on to state, correlates to functioning with a blood alcohol level of 0.08 percent, or about 70 percent mental effectiveness. These fatigued residents are reported to have a 22 percent greater risk of causing a

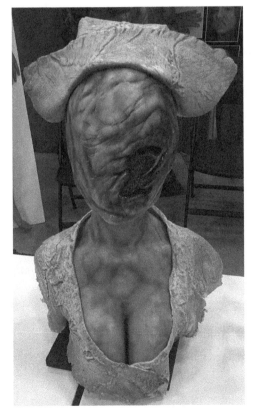

Perhaps the zombies are already walking among us in the guise of those working too many hours and overnight shifts. Pictured is a prop from artist Paul Jones's Silent Hill *display at the 2016 Niagara Falls Comic Con.*

medical error than well-rested doctors. "Imagine an intoxicated person working in a hospital setting," Frederick Southwick, professor at the University of Florida, said, "and you'll have a better understanding of the dangers of being fatigued."

Consider these facts and statistics alongside the common reaction when the average person is asked if they want to enter an abandoned, allegedly haunted hospital. Most people would be reluctant to step inside old closed hospital buildings, worried about the apparitions of long-dead patients, or speculating about the tales told about eerie moans and odd, inexplicable thumps in the night.

But most of us, when faced with a medical emergency, don't have much choice in terms of our treatment. If injured, we are rushed to the nearest hospital — where staff are likely suffering from some form of sleep deprivation due to shift work or long twelve-hour shifts.

Modern media likes to speculate about a coming zombie apocalypse, as popularized by television shows like *The Walking Dead*. But perhaps the zombies aren't coming. Perhaps they are already here.

Perhaps instead of requiring a dramatic post-apocalyptic alteration to our world to appear, the reality is that zombies are already walking among us in the guise of those working too many hours and overnight shifts, just waiting to care for us in their sleep-deprived zombielike states as we are rolled, unsuspectingly, into an emergency room.

HAUNTED PRISONS

CANADA

Cornwall Jail

Cornwall, Ontario

Built in 1833, the Cornwall Jail was operational until 2002, when the Ministry of Correctional Services closed it in favour of newer, larger facilities in major cities.

Claims suggest that as many as two hundred prisoners, who either died or were executed in the prison, were buried in the courtyard. This might be the cause of the significant paranormal activity experienced there.

The Haunted Places website states that apparitions of a woman and a child have been reported there. There are also reports of a series of disembodied voices, including one heard humming a low tune. The sounds of cell doors closing and the echo of non-existent carts moving through the empty hallways are also said to be heard.

Kingston Penitentiary

Kingston, Ontario

The Kingston Penitentiary was opened with a population of six prisoners on June 1, 1835, with an odd and dark mandate: the treatment

The Kingston Penitentiary on the shores of Lake Ontario.

would not be cruel but so otherwise irksome and terrible that during the convict's afterlife he might dread nothing so much as a return to the punishment experienced.

The most famous ghost story of this location originates in 1897 and is recounted in *Ghosts of Kingston* by Glen Shackleton. It involves two prison guards who were doing their rounds late one night when they spotted a man in convict clothing exiting a door from the penitentiary hospital and heading across the courtyard to another building. Ordering the man to halt, the two guards were startled to see the man pay no attention to their order. They watched him continue to move about the courtyard, eventually returning to the hospital door. As he reached the door, the convict turned to face the guards, and they both froze on the spot. The man they were looking at was the spitting image of a former inmate by the name of George Hewell, who had been shot and killed almost one year earlier and who had sworn as he died that he would return from the grave to make them pay for the manner in which they had wronged him.

Carleton County Gaol

Ottawa, Ontario

The last place one might seriously consider staying on a holiday would be a building that, over the course of one hundred years, has been referred to as a monstrous medieval relic with conditions far below the limits of human decency. Yet each year thousands of people delight in staying overnight in refurbished jail cells at the Ottawa Jail Hostel on Nicholas Street in downtown Ottawa. The building is considered one of the most haunted buildings in North America and appears on Lonely Planet's list of the top ten spookiest buildings around the world.

While it was technically never a hospital or asylum, the ninth floor served as a hospital for a short time before being converted into a prison area for women and children, and the mentally ill were often kept in the old Carleton County Gaol, also known as the Nicholas Street Gaol or Ottawa Jail, while waiting for space to open up in the asylum in nearby Kingston.

Living conditions at this jail have been compared to those of a medieval prison. It is a relic of the dark ages where hundreds of men, women, and children were crammed into conditions that would be unfit for animals, surrounded by filth, disease, and human waste. A combination of murderers, petty thieves, the criminally insane, and the insufferable poor were all thrown together into a motley crew of tortured inmates.

In a 1915 *Ottawa Citizen* article, a man named John Lyons wrote about the abhorrent conditions he experienced in his thirty-one-day stay at the prison, declaring it "a social hothouse, as it were, for the creation and maturing of criminals."

Lyons described one man he encountered there who had been serving his third term for vagrancy. The man, he said, was not of sound mind and had to be washed and dressed much like a baby, yet he was forced into hard labour, working daily on the stone pile. "Left to himself, he is harmless," Lyons wrote, "but when others torment him he becomes a perfect demon.

"Confining the insane in the ordinary prisons is not fair to the guards, the other prisoners, or to the insane themselves; moreover, it is a direct contravention of existing law."

When, after 110 years of operation, the Carleton County Gaol was finally closed in 1972, the last thing one might have suspected the building would become was a youth hostel. And those who stay there might not just be experiencing the unique novelty of staying in an old converted jail cell — they may end up experiencing something far deeper and darker from an encounter with one of the thousands of lost souls alleged to still wander the building for eternity.

Among the reported ghosts in this building is a woman wearing a blanket over her head like a hood. She is said to haunt the fourth-floor women's washroom, appearing in profile then disappearing just after she turns to reveal that she has no face. Some believe her spirit might be indicative of the thousands of "faceless" and "nameless" women who died and were buried in unmarked graves on the prison grounds.

Down the hallway of the old death row, a dark, robed male figure has also been spotted. He is said to glide down the hallway in his long dark cloak, making no noise, and then slowly disappear into thin air.

An eerie "vampire ghost" that drains the energy of those sensitive enough to detect it is said to haunt a back stairway. The stairway is also known as the secret staircase as it led to a tunnel that connected to the governor's house.

Of course, the most legendary ghost to appear is that of Patrick James Whelan, the man charged with the murder of Thomas D'Arcy McGee (a journalist and politician). Whelan was hanged in a public execution at the prison in front of five thousand spectators on February 11, 1869. A ghost fitting Whelan's description is said to appear to some guests either standing at the foot of their beds or sitting on the ends of them. Some have reported seeing him reading what appears to be a Bible.

Some of the paranormal phenomena that have been reported in the old jail do not involve visible spectres, but rather physical manifestations. Odd, inexplicable knocking from behind closed doors in vacant rooms has been heard, a heavy steel door once slammed shut on a staff member's hand during a guided tour of the facility, and a pair of mischievous boys fooling around on a school tour both developed simultaneous and instantaneous nosebleeds.

Knowing all this, if you ever visited Canada's capital, how likely would you be to stay overnight in this very unique accommodation? What if the already attractive and affordable price included free breakfast and complimentary WiFi? Oh yes, and the eerie ambiance of a building steeped in over 150 years of a dark and disturbing history.

Old Don Jail

Toronto, Ontario

Also known as the Toronto Jail, the Old Don Jail, which opened in 1864 and ran until 2013, is now used as the administrative wing of a rehabilitation hospital. One of the former hangmen at the prison, Arthur Bartholomew English, who operated under the name Arthur Ellis, lives on via a series of annual awards for mystery writers given out by the Crime Writers of Canada: the Arthur Ellis Awards.

Various estimates state that more than one million prisoners had called the Don Jail home by 1977, when the main building was closed as a jail operation, leaving only the east wing (which opened in 1958) to serve as the Toronto Jail. In a May 7, 2003, *Toronto Star* article, Linda Diebel wrote that it was "like walking into a madhouse from another century."

There are many eerie episodes reported here. Some visitors claimed to have been struck by bouts of inexplicable crying when inside the building. One of the most well-known spirits to haunt this building is said to be that of an inmate who hung herself in her jail cell. She is allegedly seen hovering near the main rotunda and, at times, is said to have let loose howling screams in the depths of night.

In 2007 during an archeological assessment, human remains were found on the jail's grounds, a fact that might also lead to further speculation regarding the hauntings reported there.

Pied-du-Courant Prison

Montreal, Quebec

The Pied-du-Courant Prison was the site of multiple executions, mostly of those accused of war crimes in the Patriote political movement of the Lower Canada Rebellion in 1837 and 1838. Multiple EVP recordings have turned up with voices that investigators believe belong to the hanged men.

Operated from 1836 to 1912 as the city's prison, the building stood vacant for almost a full decade before the *Société des alcools du Québec* (or SAQ, the provincial liquor board) made it their headquarters. When we're being cheeky, we might wonder if alcohol has anything at all to do with the reports of odd activity in the building.

Old abandoned prisons and hospitals are often filled with asbestos and are in such an advanced state of disrepair that high fences and warnings are needed to keep people out and protect them from hazards.

THE UNITED STATES

ARIZONA

Yuma Territorial Prison: The Unlucky Seven Spirits

Yuma

The very first seven prisoners to ever be locked into Yuma Territorial Prison were said to have constructed their own cells with their bare hands. During the more than thirty years that it was operational, more than three thousand prisoners were crowded inside the brutal prison's walls. According to Troy Taylor in an article on the American Hauntings website, more than one hundred prisoners died in that time period. Legend has it that some of them, perhaps even one of those original seven prisoners, never truly left the site.

One story shared involves a writer from *Arizona Highways* magazine who intended to write an in-depth personal experience piece for the magazine by staying for two days and two nights of research in the prison's "dark cell" area — an isolation area that had been used for the most unruly prisoners. By choice, she was chained and left with nothing but bread and water to eat. Not only didn't she last a single night, but within hours of her isolation she was calling out to the staff and begging to be let out, convinced that there was someone else in the cell with her.

The Haunted Places website reports other ghostly claims from the prison, including a spirit that pinches visitors and one that is often heard singing. These and other spirits are said to lurk within the walls of this prison. Yuma Territorial Prison originally opened in 1875 and processed prisoners until 1909, when inmates were transferred to the newly constructed Arizona State Prison Complex in nearby Florence.

CALIFORNIA

Lincoln Heights Jail

Los Angeles
Originally built in 1931 and then decommissioned in 1965, the Lincoln Heights Jail is best known as the site of what came to be known as "Bloody Christmas." The infamous incident involved the unprovoked beating of seven prisoners. The book *L.A. Confidential* was partially inspired by that incident, and parts of the movie of the same name were filmed there. Multiple films and music videos have been filmed at that location, including scenes from the 1984 horror film *A Nightmare on Elm Street* — perhaps fitting, given the fact that the building is allegedly haunted. The Bilingual Foundation of the Arts occupied the space from 1979 until 2014.

COLORADO

Museum of Colorado Prisons

Canon City
Among the phenomena reported in this location are the phantom smell of tobacco when there is nobody smoking nearby, and odd, unexplainable cold spots in various locations throughout the building, particularly within the laundry room.

A female prisoner who passed away in Cell 19 is said to linger in spectral form and audible sounds, continuing to haunt the precise spot where she died. Ghostly orbs have been reported on photographs taken in her cell, where the sound of disembodied coughing has also been heard.

CONNECTICUT

Olde Newgate Prison

East Granby
Originally a copper mine beginning in 1705, the tunnels of this location were converted into Connecticut's first prison, which operated between 1773 and 1827. Many different apparitions have been reported at this location, including one that paranormal investigators have nicknamed a "tour guide." The tour guide appears to replicate the actions of one proudly showing visitors around the place. Guests have also reported being touched by unseen hands and hearing ghostly screams echoing through the dank dark corridors.

FLORIDA

Old Jefferson County Jail

Monticello
Declared a historical site, and operating as the Monticello Old Jail Museum, the Old Jefferson County Jail was built in 1909. The local sheriff lived on the ground floor and basement of this prison while the prisoners were housed on the upper floor. People who have been inside the building claim to have heard sounds coming from the upper floor, including strange moaning and the clanking of what sounds like cell doors.

GEORGIA

The Old Tallapoosa Jail

Tallapoosa

Located underneath the chief of police's office, the area that was once the old jail is currently no more than a storage room. Witnesses have reported odd and inexplicable occurrences, including items being relocated on their own and strange noises coming from the basement cell. It is believed that two slain officers might still be making their unearthly patrols for eternity in this old jail.

IDAHO

Old Idaho Penitentiary

Boise

The Old Idaho Penitentiary was built in 1870 and held more than thirteen thousand prisoners during the course of its operation before it closed in 1973. One of the spirits believed to haunt the jail is Harry Orchard, a man who was convicted of murder.

Orchard served almost fifty years in the prison, making repeated attempts at parole that were all refused. When the inmate was finally offered parole, he refused, and he died in prison at the age of eighty-eight.

Another spirit who might be roaming the halls is that of George Hamilton, the man who designed the prison's dining hall. Upon his release Hamilton was so upset at being ordered to leave the prison that he took his own life the very same day.

Staff from the building have reported odd smells, eerie voices, flickering shadows moving past them, unexplainable cold spots, and the sounds of footsteps echoing down the vacant corridors.

INDIANA

Old Whitley Jail

Columbia City
Constructed in 1875, the Old Whitley Jail is said to be haunted by a man named Charles Butler. Butler, an alcoholic and a bully who shot his wife in the back in 1883, escaped from the prison with four other inmates, only to be recaptured when he passed out in a bar.

Butler was sentenced to be hanged, but his execution apparently didn't go off exactly as planned. When a malfunction occurred in the gallows, the man was said to have strangled for about ten minutes before he died.

Butler's ghost is blamed for malfunctioning video cameras, as well as the sudden draining of fully charged batteries in flashlights and cameras.

Disembodied footsteps, voices, and laughter have all been heard in the prison. Displays are said to have been moved when nobody was around, and the ghost of a former sheriff is said to have been seen performing his nightly rounds patrolling the jail.

KENTUCKY

The Old Nelson County Jail

Bardstown
On the site that used to serve as the Old Nelson County Jail from 1797 until 1987 stands a unique bed and breakfast operation known as Jailer's Inn Bed and Breakfast. Its website describes the Jailer's Inn as a place of wonderful and thought-provoking contrasts, and it includes beautifully decorated guest rooms within thirty-inch-thick stone walls and behind iron-barred windows.

Both staff members and guests have reported hearing the sounds of disembodied voices, footsteps, and eerily haunting crying. A video recorded overnight in November 2009 captures one of the investigators trying to address a spirit. The sound of a child humming and uttering unintelligible words can also be heard, as can the sound of a prison cell door closing.

MAINE

Maine State Prison

Warren

Apparently, the Maine State Prison isn't haunted due to some terrible event that happened there, but due to the fact that some of the equipment there was transferred and recycled when a nearby prison in Thomaston was torn down. The prison in Thomaston was reported to have been haunted, and it seems the spirits fled, attaching themselves to the equipment, when the building was levelled.

Most of the spiritual activity in the prison seems to have occurred in the Industries Building. Correction officers have reported seeing the ghostly images of former inmates — only, in this particular case, they are not former inmates from Maine State Prison, but travelling spirits.

MISSOURI

Missouri State Penitentiary

Jefferson City

Explored by more than one hundred different paranormal investigators, including the television program *Ghost Hunters*, the Missouri State Penitentiary is said to be rife with paranormal activity and hauntings. Visitors are offered ghost tours of the facilities and some have reported seeing ghostly apparitions moving about in the shadows and hearing inexplicable noises echoing in the dark.

MONTANA

Montana State Prison Museum

Deer Lodge

The site of multiple executions, riots, and violent deaths, this prison was built in 1871 and operated until the 1970s. Since then, in the museum, guests have reported the feeling of being touched and shoved by unseen hands, the unexplained sound of disembodied voices and eerie footsteps, and strange apparitions in the old solitary confinement area of the building.

NEW JERSEY

Burlington County Prison

Mount Holly

Now a museum, this prison, built in 1811 and used until 1965, is home to a floating apparition that has been described as a "legless ghost." The ghost has been seen hovering about near the entrance and out in the prison yard. The spectral form of a tall man has also been reported, seen walking around in the basement. The third floor of this prison is said to be rife with paranormal activity, including what has been described as ectoplasmic cobwebs.

This building also houses the ghost of convicted murderer Joseph Clough, who killed his mistress with a table leg. He was held in a jail cell in death row, always chained to an eye hook in the floor of the cell. Clough was eventually hanged in the 1850s, and since then his ghost has been reported by guards and other prisoners. Reports include the movement of some presence in the otherwise empty cell or hearing the rattling of chains and Clough's ghostly moaning.

During the conversion of the prison into a museum, construction workers reported various odd phenomena, such as loud inexplicable noises, screams, and voices coming from empty rooms and corridors. Also, tools and objects that they had placed down mysteriously disappeared, only to appear again on some other floor or in a different room.

NEW YORK

Calaboose Grill

Owego

The Calaboose Grill boasts American fare and cocktails served in a historical, renovated jailhouse with outdoor seating. But this grill with the slogan "Captivating Food and Drinks" might offer more than occasionally scheduled live music as something that people will talk about and remember. *Calaboose*, by the way, is Cajun slang for "jail."

The restaurant was originally the site of the Owego Town Jail, and some believe that it is haunted by former prisoners who once lived and died on the premises.

OHIO

Ohio State Reformatory

Mansfield

Also known as the Mansfield Reformatory, the Ohio State Reformatory was built between 1886 and 1910, and remained in operation until 1990. The site has been used in multiple movie and television shoots, including as the setting of the movie *The Shawshank Redemption*. Witnesses have reported seeing shadowy figures moving about in the night and hearing slamming cell doors and yelling voices. Some women who visited have reported being physically struck by unseen hands, allegedly victims of the dark spirits that reside there.

The Precinct Office Center

West Union

Now operating as the county office, this former prison location has allegedly been haunted by the same eerie spectral figure for more than one hundred years. Prisoners reported being visited and frightened in the middle of the night by a translucent figure dressed in white robes. The visitor would soundlessly float past their cells before disappearing into thin air.

PENNSYLVANIA

The Old Jail Museum

Jim Thorpe
Ghost tours are offered on the premises of the Old Jail Museum in Jim Thorpe, a borough of Carbon County, Pennsylvania. It is reported that a bloody handprint continues to reappear on the wall there, regardless of how many times the wall is scrubbed clean or painted over.

Eastern State Penitentiary

Philadelphia
As many as one hundred spirits are said to roam the Eastern State Penitentiary in Philadelphia, Pennsylvania. Among the more well-known inmates at this prison was historical figure Al Capone. Capone was allegedly visited by the ghostly apparition of James Clark, a man who was killed in the St. Valentine's Day Massacre that Capone ordered.

The most actively haunted location in this prison is Cell Block 12. Within its walls, witnesses have reported seeing shadowy masses and odd disturbing figures moving about in the shadows.

The guard tower at this prison is also said to be haunted by a former prison guard who continues to stand watch over the prison even after his death.

York Prison

York

Now abandoned, this historic prison was originally built in 1906 and was in operation until 1979. Multiple visitors have reported the eerie sensation of being followed around by the ghosts of former inmates as they moved through the building. Other reports include claims by people who have smelled cigarette smoke and seen the flickering lights of a cigarette being lit in locations where there is nobody around to have done so.

SOUTH CAROLINA

Abbeville County Museum

Abbeville

The three-storey Abbeville County Museum building was originally a jail, constructed in 1854. It remained functional as a jail until 1948. It is not surprising that the third floor is reported to be the most haunted since this is where the worst prisoners were housed. Staff at the museum claim to have encountered the ghost of a former African-American prisoner by the name of Earl, who is described as friendly in nature.

TENNESSEE

Tennessee State Prison

Nashville

The elaborate architecture of Tennessee State Prison brings to mind images of castles and fortresses. It was modelled after the penitentiary in Auburn, New York, and is both beautiful and formidable. It boasts eight hundred small cells, each of which is intended to house a single inmate, and walls that are three-feet-thick solid stone. The prison operated from 1898 to 1992 and has served as the location for multiple films of vastly different genres, including *Ernest Goes to Jail*, *The Last Castle*, and *The Green Mile*.

Multiple riots, fires, and other egregious activities occurred in this prison during its operation, including one incident where a group of inmates took control of one of the wings and held it for eighteen hours before finally surrendering. In another incident, in 1902, seventeen prisoners blew out the end of a different wing of the prison. The explosion killed one inmate and let two others escape, never to be seen within those walls again. Five years later another group of prisoners commandeered a switch engine and drove it through one of the prison's gates. And in 1938 inmates staged a mass escape.

Tennessee State Prison is considered a veritable hot spot for paranormal activity, and over the years different people have reported hearing voices, alarming yells and screams, footsteps and other unexplainable sounds.

WEST VIRGINIA

West Virginia State Penitentiary

Moundsville

West Virginia State Penitentiary is a Gothic-style prison that operated between 1876 and 1995. People believe that this prison, once considered one of the most violent in the United States, left some sort of permanent mark on the space-time fabric of the location.

Many ghost-themed shows have investigated and reported upon this site, including *Scariest Places on Earth*, *Paranormal State*, *Ghost Lab*, *Fear*, and *Ghost Adventures*.

One particular spirit reputed to haunt the building is known as the "Shadow Man," a figure composed mostly of dark and ominous shadows. It is said that he follows people around by staying hidden within the very shadows that they cast.

Based upon its dark past, mystery, and the alleged hauntings, several different types of tours are regularly held at this location: the regular Daily Tours, the evening Twilight Tours, Dungeon of Horrors and Thriller Thursdays tours, and overnight Ghost Adventures and Private Paranormal Investigations.

WYOMING

Wyoming Frontier Prison

Rawlins

Operational from 1901 to 1981, this location is touted both as the first state penitentiary and as the penitentiary that housed Wyoming's most violent criminals. Prisoners there were treated to barbaric conditions, including the use of an infamous "whipping pole" to which inmates were chained and beaten. Wyoming Frontier Prison's death row led to both gallows for hangings and gas chambers.

It is reported that more than 250 people died within the walls of this prison. This includes a prisoner who was lynched by fellow inhabitants for his abuse of an elderly townswoman, as well as those who died in fires and riots.

Investigators visiting the prison have concluded that not only is there a strong negative psychic energy trapped within the prison, but also there exists both residual and active hauntings.

Wyoming Territorial Prison Museum

Laramie

This former penitentiary — which once housed the infamous outlaw Butch Cassidy — operated as a federal penitentiary from 1872 until 1890 and as a state prison from 1890 to 1901. After that, ownership was transferred to the University of Wyoming and the site was used as an agricultural experiment station until 1989. Two years later the facility was opened to the public as a museum, and in 2004 it was designated a State Historic Site.

The smell of cigar smoke has been reported at this location, attributed to a former inmate named Julius Greenwelch. This particular prisoner was a cigar maker incarcerated in 1897 for killing his wife in a jealous rage, and his ghostly form has also appeared in the doorway of what used to be his cell. Legend has it that his ghost began to manifest only after the major renovations and restoration work began in the prison in 1989.

REST OF THE WORLD

AUSTRALIA

Hobart Penitentiary Chapel

Tasmania

The Hobart Penitentiary Chapel was built in 1831 and was intended as a place of worship for the population of settlers and convicts. As the years passed, however, the building's use and purpose continually changed, right up until it was closed in 1847 due to concerns over the inhumane conditions.

The building was modified and enhanced into a fully operational penitentiary in 1857, complete with an execution yard. As such, it was no longer considered to be a peaceful place to commune with the Lord — more like hell on earth.

The site is said to house spirits both within and outside its walls, including the spirits of the thirty-two convicted inmates sentenced to death by hanging.

Near the gallows, visitors have reported an overwhelming sense of trepidation and intense feelings of heat, regardless of the season or temperature. The sensation of being touched and grabbed by unseen hands is also commonly reported, as is the smell of decomposition and blood.

Part of the building was demolished in 1960 and then reconstructed in the spirit of the original design at a later date. Regardless of any desire to restore the old building to its once former glory, visitors report uncanny feelings of dread, hopelessness, and despair.

Those who venture inside have reported feeling both cold and hot spots, hearing the haunting sound of voices and footsteps, and seeing eerie spectral visions of former prisoners moving through the shadows. Some people have been so overwhelmed by oppressive feelings within those walls that they've had to leave in order to escape the painful headaches and difficulty breathing that they experienced.

UNITED KINGDOM AND IRELAND

Kilmainham Gaol

Dublin, Ireland

Now a museum run by the office of public works, the Kilmainham Gaol is considered one of the most important Irish monuments of the modern period. One of the largest unoccupied prisons in Europe, it was first constructed in 1796. Because it was seen as a site of oppression in which women, men, and children suffered under extremely poor conditions, the prison was closed in 1924.

Doors within the building are said to open and close on their own, ghostly footsteps are said to echo down empty corridors, and lights go off and on all by themselves. Visitors report having been touched by cold invisible hands, and the chapel reported to be full of an especially evil force.

Bodmin Jail

Cornwall, England

Built in 1779 by prisoners of war, the Bodmin Jail was the first British prison to keep prisoners in individual cells. The first hanging in this prison took place in 1785 and over the century and a half it was operational, more than fifty public hangings took place there.

While some parts of the old jail have been refurbished over the years, parts of it remain in ruins, casting a foreboding gloom over the whole place. Simple, gory exhibitions have been created with crude mannequins, and plaques describing particular offences and punishments for the former inmates are available for tourists to read. A popular ghost walk is available in the evening for visitors to learn even more speculative and gruesome tales associated with the prison.

The ghost of Selina Wadge, a woman hanged for drowning her child, is said to be one of the most infamous spirits to haunt the prison. It is reported that pregnant women, in particular, are sometimes overcome with emotion when walking through certain spots.

Clink Prison Museum

London, England

The Clink was voted the most notorious medieval prison for its horrible conditions and the outrageously grizzly interrogation and torture methods used on prisoners. Upon entering the oldest prison in England, people occasionally report being overcome with a foreboding feeling of dread and gloom, and noises such as the rattling of chains or glass breaking can be heard echoing through the empty passageways. Apparently, objects being physically moved by way of poltergeist activity have also been reported here.

For those who believe the name of this location might have something to do with the slang used to describe a prison or a jail cell, indeed, it appears that is the case. The name itself was likely onomatopoeic in nature, derived from the sound of metal striking against metal as a jail cell door closes, or perhaps even the sound of the chains the prisoners wore rattling against one another.

Crumlin Road Jail

Belfast, Northern Ireland

Operational between 1845 and 1996, Crumlin Road Jail is now a tourist attraction. The B-wing of this prison is where the face of a man has reportedly been captured in a famous photograph, and the spirit of a former warden allegedly still patrols the halls of this wing. In the C-wing, the ghost of another walking man is often seen, only to disappear moments after he is spotted. And over in the D-wing a ghostly apparition has been seen standing in a particular doorway, casually watching visitors pass by.

The Tolbooth

Aberdeen, Scotland

Responsible for the burning of witches under King James VI, the Tolbooth Museum is often cited as one of the most haunted buildings in Aberdeen. Originally built between 1616 and 1629, it was once a prison, and it is believed that the ghosts of the victims burned there haunt the building as do other former inmates. Ghostly whispers, eerie footsteps, and strange shadows have been reported here, as well as the spirit of a short man dressed in 1920s clothing — one of the newer spirits on the site!

Beaumaris Gaol

Beaumaris, Wales

With over thirty thousand visitors per year to its museum, the Beaumaris Gaol is a popular attraction. It was built in 1829 and remained in use until 1878. Before becoming a museum the building served as a police station, as well as a children's clinic. Only two men were ever executed in the prison's relatively short run, and both were buried within the walls of the jail in a lime pit. While the exact location of the burial plots remains unknown, the prison is said to be haunted by the second man who was hanged there, a man who proclaimed his innocence to his very last breath. Legend has it that the man, Richard Rowlands, cursed the church clock in one of his final statements, saying that the four different faces of this clock would never again show the same time. Since then it is reported that the clock faces have never properly aligned.

Ruthin Gaol

Ruthin, Wales

The Ruthin Gaol was constructed in 1775 and was operational until 1916. Even though only a single prisoner was ever executed in this location, that prisoner, a William Hughes, is said to haunt it. Visitors report having seen the ghost in the condemned man's former cell and occasionally being touched. The spirit apparently has a preference for touching women who visit.

CONCLUSION

Of any of the possible locations in the world that are ripe for paranormal activity or prone to visitation of spirits from beyond this mortal realm, hospitals are among the most likely, charged with the type of energy exchanged when life begins and ends.

What other buildings or institutions have been created for the purpose of life, whether it be to bring new life into the world, via childbirth, or ushering life out, via unexpected and untimely deaths, or long, drawn-out palliative care situations? (Admittedly, childbirth often happens naturally outside a hospital; however, in Western culture, the association between giving birth and a hospital maternity ward is still quite strong.)

We come into the world via hospitals. We leave the world via hospitals. Life is often sustained in hospitals. The energy and force and power of such places must be, if one considers such things, absolutely tremendous.

Alongside those institutions designed to provide medical care, surgical treatment, and nursing care for the sick and injured are psychiatric institutions, psychiatric hospitals, and asylums, which specialize in the healing and treatment of mental illnesses. At a time when we knew so much less about the mind and believed in all sorts of connections between the human brain and external factors — the term "lunatic" derives from the Latin term for "moon," one of those external factors, and is a derogatory term to describe someone suffering from a mental illness

Throughout history, there has been a astonishingly thin line between the treatment afforded to those consigned to insane asylums and those sentenced to prison terms.

or deficiency — treatments for mental conditions often included acts we now consider morally reprehensible.

Throughout history there has been an eerily thin grey line drawn between insane asylums and prisons. During certain periods the line was so thin that rehabilitation of either a criminal mind or a mentally ill mind was virtually impossible. The perceived solution was often merely the act of locking certain types of people away from the rest of society, a dog's breakfast of inmates massed together.

Particularly in such holding areas, where anxiety, confusion, tension, mental illness, criminal tendencies, and an overall sense of hopelessness reigned supreme, the return of the spectral seems likely. According to one definition of a haunted space, such conditions might leave permanent wrinkles and impressions on the very fabric of time.

Throughout this book, we have examined locales through various stages in their history, studied many of the people who lived and worked in those spaces, and researched those who died there. After engaging with so many stories that play upon our fears of the dark and of the unknown, some might feel a sense of despair, anxiety, and fear. While we respectfully acknowledge the many sad tales and tragic circumstances that have been documented on the previous pages, we like to also think that reading such stories can be inspiring.

Asking the inevitable question "what if?" and wondering about the phenomena we have seen ourselves or read about in others' experiences makes us pause, speculate, and consider life and death, the universe, and our place in it. We hope we've laid out some stories that make you think, question, wonder, and imagine.

Albert Einstein said, "Imagination is more important than knowledge." Knowledge is limited to all that we know and currently understand, while imagination embraces the entire world and all that there will ever be to know and understand. He also said, "The most beautiful thing we can experience is the mysterious."

Rhonda and I truly hope that you have experienced the mysterious while reading the preceding pages and that it has prompted your imagination and your sense of wonder.

— *Mark Leslie*

FURTHER READING

Books

Belanger, Jeff. *Encyclopedia of Haunted Places: Ghostly Locales from Around the World*. Edison, NJ: Castle Books, 2005.

Belyk, Robert C. *Ghosts: True Tales of Eerie Encounters*. Victoria: Horsdal & Schubert, 2002.

Coren, Stanley. *Sleep Thieves: An Eye-Opening Exploration into the Science and Mysteries of Sleep*. New York: Simon & Schuster, 1996.

Crowe, Catherine. *The Night Side of Nature; Or, Ghosts and Ghost Seers, Vol II*. London: T.C. Newby, 1848.

Jeffries, Benjamin S. *Lost in the Darkness: Life Inside the World's Most Haunted Prisons, Hospitals, and Asylums*. Atglen, PA: Schiffer, 2013.

Leslie, Mark. *Creepy Capital: Ghost Stories of Ottawa and the National Capital Region*. Toronto: Dundurn, 2016.

Leslie, Mark, and Jenny Jelen. *Spooky Sudbury: True Tales of the Eerie and Unexplained*. Toronto: Dundurn, 2013.

Shackleton, Glen. *Ghosts of Kingston: From the Files of the Haunted Walk*. Vancouver: Trafford, 2008.

———. *Ghosts of Ottawa*. Vancouver: Trafford, 2008.

Sutherland, Joel A. *Haunted Canada 4: More True Tales of Terror*. Toronto: Scholastic Canada, 2014.

Vernon, Steve. *Halifax Haunts: Exploring the City's Spookiest Spaces*. Halifax: Nimbus, 2009.

Waters, Stephanie. *Ghosts of Colorado Springs and Pikes Peak*. Charleston: History Press, 2012.

Websites

Abandoned Whereabouts — https://abandonedwhereabouts.com

American Hauntings — www.prairieghosts.com

Bedford Paranormal — www.bedfordparanormal.com

Coast to Coast AM — www.coasttocoastam.com

Exemplore — http://exemplore.com

Haunted Places — www.hauntedplaces.org

Mysterious Heartland — https://mysteriousheartland.com

Paranormal Database — www.paranormaldatabase.com

PSICAN (Paranormal Studies and Inquiry Canada) — www.psican.org

Unexplained Mysteries of the World — http://real-ghosts-webs.blogspot.com

The Workhouse — www.workhouses.org.uk

ACKNOWLEDGEMENTS

A Word About the Selected Sources

Rhonda's Notes

It wouldn't feel right to end this book without saying something about the sources I used in putting my part together. For good or for ill.

There was one book I consumed, reading it cover to cover more than once. I could not get enough of *Lost in the Darkness: Life Inside the World's Most Haunted Prisons, Hospitals, and Asylums* by Benjamin S. Jeffries. When I began researching this book, I borrowed *Lost in the Darkness* from the library and started reading it. I was reading it in my leisure time, though, so I had several other books on the go, too. When *Lost in the Darkness* was due back three weeks later, I wasn't quite finished. So I renewed it. And then again. And when it was due the third time, I couldn't renew it again — local library rules. And so began a cycle that lasted for months. I would renew the book twice, return it to the library, where they would check it in, and then I would immediately check it back out. Again, I'd renew it twice before taking it back.... You see where I'm going with this. I especially appreciated that Jeffries had been to many of the places he was writing about and was therefore able to give his personal impressions of them.

Lacking the ability to travel that extensively myself, I often relied on paranormal investigation reality shows to help me form an impression of the hospitals I was writing about. As I mentioned in the Introduction, I come to the paranormal from a skeptical place, so some of the more hyperbolic episodes of these shows would make me facepalm or talk back to the screen, but they were incredibly helpful in depicting the places I was writing about. And some of the experiments performed or footage caught on camera were fascinating. So for that I am incredibly grateful.

This brings me to Ben Myckan and Rona Anderson. Ben and Rona are paranormal investigators from Edmonton, who braved ridiculously cold temperatures to meet with me and share the stories of their encounters within the Charles Camsell Hospital. The Camsell was the inspiration for this whole book, and without Ben and Rona that section would have been far less interesting. They were a lot of fun to talk to, and had tons of great stories about the things they've seen and done. I wouldn't be surprised someday to see their names on the spine of a book in the paranormal section of the library.

I also need to recognize Kat Hayes for all the wonderful research material she provided. I am still going through the massive sheath of papers, and I may yet do something awesome with them. Only time will tell. Thank you also to Jocelyn for sharing her Camsell hospital story with me.

These acknowledgements wouldn't be complete without shining a spotlight on the team at Dundurn. Every step of the way they have been amazingly professional and helpful. This book would not be the thing of awesomeness that it is without all their skill and hard work. Thank you. Thank you. Thank you.

Finally, thank you, Mark. I appreciate your willingness to show me the non-fiction ropes. Your sense of humour, lack of ego, and work ethic have made what could have been a very trying experience (so! much! research!) an awful lot of fun. We'll have to do it again sometime.

Acknowledgements

Mark's Notes

Without a few key words that Rhonda uttered to me at a writers' conference, this book wouldn't exist. Those words led the two of us down an intriguing path.

When Rhonda and I first found ourselves brainstorming about the possibility of working on a book about haunted hospitals, I never imagined how enriching the experience could be. I didn't foresee that she wouldn't just be a co-author on this project, but an inspiring and driving force to keep the project on track. Rhonda's approach, her good humour, and her relentlessness in the face of adversity are just a few of the traits that made it a pleasure and a thrill to work on this book together — although, admittedly, because we're in different provinces, "together" has meant two in-person meetings and a lot of instant messages and email.

Whenever I begin a new paranormal project, the first set of books I turn to are those by John Robert Colombo, who is known as Canada's "Master Gatherer." John's books are not only intriguing, chilling, and frightening, but they remain among my most precious for inspiration. While the content of this book doesn't reflect much of John's, I regularly returned to his books to consult their style, approach, and overall demeanour on the topics we covered.

As in my previous book of ghost stories about Ottawa, I relied on the writings and research of Glen Shackleton, founder of Haunted Walks Inc. (www.hauntedwalk.com). I regularly consulted Glen's books *Ghosts of Ottawa* and *Ghosts of Kingston* as I was fleshing out particular chapters for this volume.

Another volume I found particularly fun to browse and consult is *Encyclopedia of Haunted Places*, a compilation of ghostly locales from around the world edited by Jeff Belanger.

A great place to start when looking for haunted places to write about is often the very handy Haunted Places website (www.hauntedplaces.org).

So many different people took the time to share stories. I cannot reveal all of their names, but I would like to thank them for reaching out and telling their stories. In particular, I'd like to thank Belinda Crowson of the Galt Museum and Archives for sharing her stories and writing.

Thanks to everyone behind the scenes at Dundurn, especially the wonderful editorial team. Particular thanks go to Kate Unrau, Dominic Farrell, and Cheryl Hawley for their never-ending patience and editorial support to help make the words and stories we share as rich as possible. Thank you to the promotions folks, especially Jaclyn Hodsdon, for her relentless championing and connections that will go on even after the book is out in the wild. Carrie Gleason and her team have taken such good care of us throughout the entire process of putting this beautiful book together (including through our hemming and hawing about the brilliant cover options). Thanks to Margaret Bryant and the awesome sales team — the adventurers fighting for retail shelf spaces and talking our stories up to retail buyers. Cheers and a tip of the hat to Beth Bruder, who was responsible for that first spark of interest in these types of books, inspiring that original pitch for *Haunted Hamilton*. And where would any of us Dundurn authors be without the ongoing guidance of Sheila Douglas?

In particular, I'd like to thank my partner, Liz, for so many things: for accompanying me on in-person tours of locations to be used in this book; for helping with atmospheric reference, talking to locals, and taking photographs; and for listening while I debated aloud about how to approach a particular story and tried to sound out a particular perspective or "take" on a tale. And it goes without saying how much I appreciate Liz doing all of the driving during the Ottawa and Kingston research while I, under a tight deadline, typed madly in the passenger seat. I know she always has my back.

IMAGE CREDITS

BY THE SAME AUTHOR

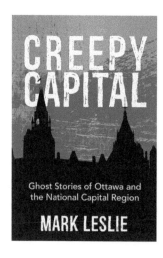

Creepy Capital
Mark Leslie

A supernatural tour of the Ottawa region with ghostwatcher Mark Leslie as your guide.

Come along with paranormal raconteur Mark Leslie as he uncovers first-person accounts of ghostly happenings throughout Ottawa and the surrounding towns — the whole region is rife with ghostly encounters and creepy locales.

Discover the doomed financier who may be haunting the Château Laurier. Experience the eerie shadows and sounds at the Bytown Museum. Listen to the echoing howls of former prison inmates at the Nicholas St. Hostel. And feel the bitter sadness of the ghost of Watson's Mill in Manotick. You'll marvel at the multitude of ghosts that walk the streets and historic landmarks of Canada's capital.

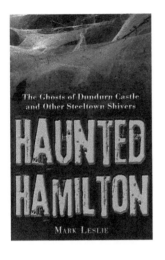

Haunted Hamilton

Mark Leslie

2013 Hamilton Arts Council Literary Award
— Shortlisted, Nonfiction

Hamilton, Ontario, may seem just like any other city,
but a haunted past is hidden beneath it.

From the Hermitage ruins to Dundurn Castle, from the Customs House to Stoney Creek Battlefield Park, the city of Hamilton, Ontario, is steeped in a rich history and culture. But beneath the surface of the Steel City there dwells a darker heart — from the shadows of yesteryear arise the unexplainable, the bizarre, and the chilling.

Lock the doors and turn on all the lights before you settle down with this book, because once you begin to read about the supernatural elements that lurk within this seemingly normal city in Southern Ontario, strange bumps in the night will take on new, more sinister meanings. Prepare to be thrilled and chilled with this collection of tales compiled from historical documents, first-person accounts, and the files of the paranormal group Haunted Hamilton, which has been investigating and celebrating Hamilton's historic haunted past since 1999.

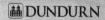